WITH THE HAND

WITH THE HAND

A Cultural History of Masturbation

Mels Van Driel

Translated by Paul Vincent

REAKTION BOOKS

Published by Reaktion Books Ltd
33 Great Sutton Street
London EC1V ODX, UK

www.reaktionbooks.co.uk

First published 2012

First published in 2010 as *Met de hand. Een culturele geschiedenis van de soloseks*
by Uitgeverij De Arbeiderspers, Amsterdam

Translated by Paul Vincent

English-language translation © Reaktion Books, 2012

This publication has been made possible with financial support from the
Dutch Foundation for Literature.

Printed and bound in Great Britain by TJ International, Padstow, Cornwall

British Library Cataloguing in Publication Data
Driel, Mels van, 1954–
    With the hand : a cultural history of masturbation.
    1. Masturbation.
    I. Title
    306.7'72-dc23

ISBN 978 1 86189 919 4

Contents

1

Introduction

Masturbation refers to the practice of stimulating one's own genitalia in such a way as to produce sexual arousal and possibly orgasm. In the case of a man this means that his semen is not deposited in the appropriate orifice in a woman's body. He wastes his seed, in the centuries-old view of many religions and cultures.

Other popular terms for this activity are onanism, auto-eroticism, solitary sex and, more recently, sex for one. The phenomenon occurs in humans and animals and in both sexes. 'Masturbation' derives from the Latin words *mas* and *turbare*, 'masculine/masculinity' and 'move (violently)'. A variant of this etymology interprets the first part of the word as a form of *manus*, 'hand', and the second as *stuprum*, 'debauch'. The Latin poet Martial uses the form *masturbor*, i.e. as a *deponent* verb, which is passive in form and active in meaning. The active form *masturbare* is not found.

Slang terms for the practice of masturbation are legion and often very inventive. Besides the familiar British 'wank' and American 'jerk off', websites like www.nowscape.com yield literally hundreds of picturesque expressions for masturbation, male and female. For men these include: assault on a friendly weapon, being your own best friend, charming the cobra, Custer's last stand, getting in touch with yourself, one man show, playing the organ, punishing the bishop, roughing up the suspect and shaking hands with Abe Lincoln. Women have a slightly more limited choice (though some examples, like 'getting in touch with your-self', are clearly unisex): a general term is 'fingering (oneself)', while others include a night with the girls, engaging in safe sex, having sex with someone you love, manual override, parting the Red Sea and squeezing the peach. A possible explanation for this imbalance in terminology is that while the genitalia form an integral part of a woman's body, the phallus is an external organ, literally and figuratively 'out on a limb'.

The very first surviving description of female masturbation is by the French writer Restif de la Bretonne, quoted by Havelock Ellis (1859–1939) in *The Evolution of Modesty* (Part I of *Studies in the Psychology of Sex*, 1897). In 1755 Restif had met a woman, not pretty but well-endowed, who had been brought up in a convent. He saw her becoming excited as she looked lustfully out of the window at a young man:

> Her movements became agitated, I approached her and am convinced that she was using terms of endearment; she had gone red. Then she sighed deeply and stood motionless, stretch-ing out her legs, which were stiff as if she were in pain . . .

Today there are excellent non-pornographic sites showing images and sounds of masturbating men and women. My own favourite is www.beautifulagony.com. On payment of a subscription one can see moving images of almost a thousand faces. The precise method of masturbation is not shown. Anyone can send in a digital video, again on payment of a fee. The contributors' names are withheld, though the exact number of minutes and megabytes taken up by their heavenly experiences are not. Obviously many people have exhibitionistic tendencies, but the site itself could be called prudish, since as was said, no genitalia are on view – not as much as a nipple. A better site for physical detail is www.seemen masturbate.com. The orgasms on www.beautifulagony.com, un-like those on many porn sites, are real. It is as if that authenticity is the payoff for the absence of breasts, vulvas, buttocks and penises. The high degree of realism excites the curiosity!

Despite the common denominator of lip-biting, groaning, etc., there is plenty of variety. Some people run their fingers through their hair, some cry, some yell. There seems to be a preference for as 'big' an orgasm as possible: the more exuberant and noisier the better. Goodbye shame.

In the cramped frames on www.beautifulagony.com things occasionally appear that give the orgasms a domestic flavour, for example, shampoo bottles on the edge of the bath and pillowslips with a ship pattern on them. Telephones ring and are sometimes even answered. 'Hi, Dad.' It's hard to imagine a more respectable form of porn!

One journalist counted 965 faces on the website, 1,930 eyes, 965 noses, 1,930 ears, 965 mouths, about a hundred arms, a few pairs of glasses, rather more piercings, two Mohicans and 965 smiles. On the site faces are arranged next to each other like postage stamps, page after page, and they differ as faces always do – big noses, thin lips, pursed lips, laughing eyes, bags, freckles, light skin, dark skin, soft cheeks, moustache, goatee, a resemblance to an actor, an Adam's apple, a Keith Richards. Yet there has been some pre-selection; it's not a cross-section of the population. There are no children or elderly people, over-40s are rare, dyed hair normal. They could be passport photos for student cards, in a subject taken by more women than men, say art history or psychology.

Very occasionally masturbation is an oblique issue in politics. In 2009 a joke circulated in England relating to odd expenses claims by high-ranking politicians. What had happened? The husband of the country's first female home secretary, Jacqui Smith, had rented a number of porn movies, which, it was maintained, had subsequently been inadvertently added to the minister's claim for internet services. On 29 March 2009 Smith, who had already been severely criticized for treating her actual family house in Redditch as a 'second home' and her sister's London residence as her main base, thus enabling her to claim expenses for the more expensive location, was forced to resign from the government. Subsequently the husband was accused of having 'ruined her career single-handedly'! Smith loyally refused to condemn her partner's liking for porn, and instead produced a BBC radio documentary, 'Porn Again', examining the state of the industry, highlighting the unprecedented accessibility of pornography today and in the process, she maintained, becoming less judgemental.

Back to our main theme: masturbation is definitely not a standard topic of conversation. Perhaps because there is so little of interest to be said about it? One may even wonder if counts as 'sex'. In American education programmes for the prevention of AIDS and pregnancy it was fashionable for a while to present masturbation to teenagers as a safer choice than sex – a sop when recommending abstinence.

Of course it didn't work. One activity bears little relation to the other. Whatever one understands by sex, it is at any rate more social than masturbating. According to some, masturbation is more like picking scabs or squeezing pimples. That, by the way, says a lot about those making such assertions.

Take a party where everyone's having a good time. Add eight or so bottles of good white wine. A close-knit group of about six friends who have known each other for years and who at the end of the evening are still grouped in a tight circle. Via mortgage interest relief, the new iPod and the holiday in South Africa this kind of birthday conversation naturally gravitates towards more intimate areas: Bill's calcified nails, Kate's vaginismus, Harry's severe constipation and Melanie's experiments with the pee spout (a cardboard 'watering can' for women). And just when you think all inhibitions are gone and anything is up for discussion, the words 'jerking off' are used ('Three times a day, my friend!), and the mood changes. 'Now, now, Wim,' says the hostess, 'that's enough of that kind of talk.' Conclusion: masturbation tends to be avoided as a topic of conversation. This involves some strange assumptions: many women think men discuss it among themselves in their macho, bragging, shameless way, while men think women talk about it together, and are much more open about bodily matters than men. In practice we find that both groups are tight-lipped about it, women even more so than men. The only exception is boys in puberty.

A colleague who was at an English boarding school as an adolescent told me about the game of 'soggy biscuit'. This required the boys to masturbate together around a biscuit. When they ejaculated the aim was to land their sperm on the biscuit. The last one to come had to eat up the soggy biscuit. My colleague refused to divulge any further details, though he did say that many boys at boarding school ejaculate into a woollen sock, to avoid staining the sheets.

A celebrated sexologist once claimed in an interview that not only did between 90 and 100 per cent of adolescent boys masturbate, but that there was also widespread mutual exploration and horseplay, with a marked competitive element: who's got the biggest one, who can shoot first and furthest? Fortunately he overstated the situation with the other sex in the opposite direction. 'Girls in the same age group swoon over Mills & Boon-type fiction.' The sexologist was the Chief Officer of Health Care for Young People in the Netherlands. Himself a homosexual, his views on the acceptance of homosexuals proved over-optimistic. Sometimes the topics with which this high-profile official concerned himself were relatively innocent, like head lice in schools and vaccination in strictly religious areas, but mostly they were more sensitive, like drug use, paedophilia and homosexuality. One of his actions as Chief Officer was particularly striking. In the early 1970s there was a pop concert in Rotterdam, which the sexologist studied at close range. Afterwards he made a laconic statement about drug use. 'The problem of alcohol has been hidden under the umbrella of drug use.' On homosexuality he was progressive, and made it clear that it is not a disease. He was anxious to impress on parents that there was nothing wrong if their child came home and announced that they were gay or lesbian. He adapted a 1970s gay 'bible', which described in uncomplicated terms the joys and problems of gay life, and in the preface he expressed the hope that problems like guilt would have disappeared within ten years.

Everything was completely different back in the 1950s. On the cover of *Timelessly Old-Fashioned*, a book published in 2009 by the Dutch humorist Kees van Kooten (1941) is a picture of the shapely naked figure of Lorraine Burnette, an English glamour model who for years was his favourite 'wet-dream woman'. It is a photo from the 1950s, the period of romanticism par excellence. A time when life was still manageable and people were thoughtful and spoke nicely. Without the internet, masturbation still required a lot of effort, and there was no sex education of any kind. Van Kooten discovered late that he could take things into his own hands. 'These days boys can masturbate in comfort, with their mind-boggling array of aids, none of which were available when I was the same age as today's youngsters', sighed the writer in an interview.

In any case there is an obvious taboo on masturbation: an authoritative 2003 survey showed that as regards sexual taboos, masturbation is indisputably in first place for both men and women. Erectile problems and sexually transmitted diseases were in second and third place. Women generally enjoy talking, but when it comes to masturbation more of them find the topic difficult than do men (47 per cent as opposed to 32 per cent). The reason? In general men are more familiar with their sexual organs, for the simple reason that from an early age they encounter their penis when urinating. Girls have to conduct an active search to find out what everything looks like down below. That often does not happen, with the result that they continue to regard their genitalia as something dirty and ugly. Boys have their own worries, and when they are older they wonder whether a curved penis comes from too much jerking off. They don't usually progress to deeper existential questions.

The same 2003 survey included a question on what phenomenon in modern society should definitely cease to be taboo. What was the result concerning the silence surrounding masturbation? Only 8 per cent of women and 16 per cent of men felt that the taboo on masturbation should be lifted. Conclusion: the taboo is unlikely to be abolished. Is that a bad thing? So what if a small amount of seed is wasted by men in masturbation? 'And don't forget the trees felled for the millions of paper tissues,' you sometimes hear said in jest. That is much less applicable to women. True, some women do ejaculate, but compared with men the volumes are negligible.

Does it matter – physically – whether someone masturbates or not? Well, for women it makes little or no difference. They should simply exercise caution with strange objects, and the same obviously applies to men. Apart from that men must be careful not to be too violent, or they risk a penis fracture. This involves not breaking a bone, but rupturing the *tunica albuginea*, a tight capsule around the spongy body of the penis. Because of the thickness and tightness of this casing of connective tissue the rupture is sometimes accompanied by a snapping sound.

Another problem that can occur is the so-called 'pipe-cleaner syndrome'. This involves a rather painful subcutaneous strand in the penis, caused by thrombosis in the subcutaneous vein due to masturbation. Fortunately this usually clears up by itself.

In itself it stands to reason that the habit of masturbation can lead to a certain passivity. But what's wrong with that? For many people an active, mutually satisfying sex life is bound up with self-esteem and hence far from idyllic. All in all, however, it is not a good idea for men to masturbate five times in quick succession. The seminal vesicles empty and finally all that comes out is a little liquid or, in the worst case, blood.

Apart from that, after fourteen days of complete abstinence – no masturbation or coitus – the sperm cells will find their own way out via the urine. This is necessary, since in a healthy young man some 1,500 cells per second are produced.

'Can masturbation do any harm? No. Does it do any good? For a brief moment, but apart from that it's a rather daft activity,' a columnist once wrote. 'Daft – the way you down a chocolate éclair or two hotdogs by yourself, and call it supper.' Who would want to contradict her? Well actually, *I* would. Perhaps many people masturbate with their loved one's image in front of them. So isn't that love? A lesser kind of love? What is 'love'? For many people masturbating may be a way of loving themselves, but that has not yet been researched. Of course, if a person can share sexuality with someone else that is a bonus, but the chance of finding someone with whom you can get on well in that area for a lifetime is less than that of getting on with yourself. And you cannot argue that someone does it by himself because he or she is not capable of forming relationships. Who says that assertion is correct? We should stop reacting with supposed shock when masturbation comes up in conversation. Perhaps we should encourage it, since for many people it is just as enjoyable and healthy as those hot dogs! Moreover, many people are unaware that masturbation, like coitus, is a good cure for hiccups (Peleg and Peleg 2000)!

I am convinced that many people, old and young, educated and uneducated, still suffer from the taboo on masturbation. On Friday 9 January 2009 the Dutch Society for Sexual Medicine held its annual general meeting, which proved a memorable occasion. Its theme was 'Sex and Science'. The last speaker was Professor Wubbo Ockels, the first Dutch astronaut, whose topic was 'sex in space'. The audience was spellbound. The professor omitted to mention 'Rocket Man (I Think it's Going to be a Long, Long Time)' by Elton John and Bernie Taupin, which among other things describes how astronauts pass the time (*Rocket man burning out his fuse up here alone . . .*). However, he did demonstrate that astronauts cannot possibly have sexual intercourse. Only at the end of his talk did he mention the special space sleeping bag, his own personal design, 'which the Russians still use', 'in which your hands had some freedom of movement . . .', and as a finale he confessed that he had once 'done *it*'. The M-word did not pass his lips, though he did remark that in space 'you had to be careful with liquids . . .' Some poets express themselves in the same way, as if their bodies ejaculate litres of sperm, and they might bring about a deluge!

After hearing Ockels I decided to write this book. Perhaps I might be able to put paid to the taboo on masturbation. Or at least put paid to all kinds of nonsense about masturbation. I began by reading bulky works by historians and sociologists. What a disappointment! I found that one of the historians ended his book, dry as dust and hundreds of pages long, with the conclusion that he didn't know the answer and that the question of why masturbation was a taboo should be left to the psychologists. That doesn't get us very far. What is the solution? To extract a few pages from my book *Manhood*, surf the internet and explore libraries to consult theologians, historians, classicists, doctors, sexologists, art connoisseurs, artists, philosophers, poets, musicians and feminists, and to weld everything into a narrative. It starts off cheerfully, but unfortunately ends in a minor key. The chapters on writers, poets and artists are intended for true culture lovers of both sexes.

2

Ages, Locations and Frequencies

Does everyone do it? Or has every one done it? The answer is yes! For some people, masturbation is actually the high point of their day. The celebrated gynaecologist Hector Treub put it succinctly: 'We've all masturbated and those who say they've never done it, are still doing it!' His pronouncement was undoubtedly inspired by two famous German psychologists. Professor Berger had written long before: 'Masturbation is such a widespread activity that 99% of young men and women indulge in it on a temporary basis and the hundredth, the pure person, is hiding the truth.' Moll's comment was: 'Those who deny they have ever masturbated, have often simply forgotten.'

Small children

It is not only the sexually mature who masturbate: small children also stimulate themselves. Two-year-olds often do it by rhythmically tensing and relaxing their closed legs. Hands are sometimes also used. The Danish researchers Hansen and Balslev analysed video footage of two boys and eleven girls and observed them exerting pressure on their nappies, sometimes with their hands and sometimes with toys. Small children are sometimes quite wrongly referred to a children's neurologist because of suspected epileptic attacks, when the movement pattern indicates masturbation, often combined with sweating, flushing and hyperventilation.

This activity peaks around the age of five. Occasionally masturbation is an expression of negative emotions. Child psychiatrists regard it as abnormal if children of that age touch other children's genitals, let alone those of adults, with their mouths. The same applies to French kissing, simulated sexual intercourse and the insertion of objects in the vagina or anus.

These little children discover that 'ordinary' masturbation gives a pleasant sensation. It is different from masturbation later in life in which the object is generally to achieve orgasm. Parents are usually concerned about masturbation in their young children, but the phenomenon is perfectly normal.

In one of her books the well-known writer and psychologist Yvonne Kroonenberg describes a scene involving child masturbation:

> I was visiting a young family. The parents and I were drinking tea at the kitchen table, the eldest son was playing outside and their six-year-old daughter was lying on the sofa masturbating. You couldn't see clearly, as she was lying full length rocking on her tummy, but her father knew what she was doing.
>
> 'Stop it, Marie!' he said nonchalantly. The mother glanced at the sofa and shrugged her shoulders. 'When she was three,' she said apologetically, 'she had a teddy bear that she squeezed between her legs. We don't forbid it, but we discourage her sometimes. It looks so odd.'

Kroonenberg adds that she sees nothing wrong in it. 'It'll help her to find her way around and it's best to learn certain things early.'

Not everyone agrees with her, as is shown by the scandal over a sex-obsessed toddler, who in 2007 hit the headlines in the Netherlands' biggest daily. Great consternation had been caused at a Catholic primary school when it emerged that a four-year-old girl from Group 1 had repeatedly forced a six-year-old girl from Group 3 to perform extreme sexual acts. The four-year-old was reported to have threatened the victim and also made advances to other pupils. However, the girl, who lived in a foster-family with her little brother, was still in class without any form of help or supervision. Alarmed parents were reported to have forbidden their children to shower with the girl after PE. One angry mother claimed that the school was trying to hush the matter up: 'It's scandalous, because not only the victim but the culprit needs help and supervision. The child knows all about masturbation. That can't be normal, can it?'

A member of the board of governors stated that the school doctor would be looking into the matter, but made no further comment . . .

Young people

Many modern sex education books suggest that masturbation is a good way of discovering one's own body. In that way, they argue, the adolescent is better prepared when he or she starts having sex with a partner. That seems to imply that masturbation is fine, but is unnecessary once one is in a relationship. This has its roots in a sex education book from 1971. The author was a psychiatrist and, like almost all the founding fathers of Dutch sexology, of Jewish extraction. This is probably linked to the fact that in Jewish, unlike Christian, culture sexuality was regarded as something positive. In any case before the Second World War people with sexual problems went to a Jewish doctor, who had grown up in a culture where it was permissible to enjoy sex, albeit on certain conditions.

The psychiatrist ends his long chapter on masturbation as follows:

> If someone is married or has a permanent relationship and there is normal sexual intercourse, it is odd for one of the partners to continue masturbating alone. This will definitely signal that there is something wrong with their sexual relations. What that is can only be sensed and perhaps expressed

by the man or woman. In the vast majority of cases masturbation in marriage means that something is wrong.

That was written less than forty years ago.

According to a sex manual published in 2005, about 30 per cent of children between twelve and fourteen have some experience of masturbation. Boys start earlier. Not until the age of seventeen have more than half of girls experienced masturbation, while that applies to half of boys by the age of fourteen. It is striking that a marked difference in masturbatory behaviour can be observed between young people with different educational levels: fourteen and fifteen-year-olds with low educational qualifications masturbate less often than those who are better educated. The difference can be easily traced back to the fact that by that age those with low qualifications have already begun sexual intercourse. Cultural background is also a factor: boys from the Antilles appear to be more experienced, while those with dual Dutch and Moroccan nationality are relatively the least experienced. Among girls we find that those with a Turkish background are even less experienced than Moroccan girls, but Surinamese and Antillean girls report that they masturbate relatively infrequently. This is linked to the powerful resistance to masturbation in Muslim culture.

We know from a 1990 survey that 80 per cent of boys aged fourteen and fifteen masturbate, and after that the percentage rises to 90. If one compares those figures with the statistics in the 2005 survey it becomes clear that there has been a sharp rise between the ages of twelve and fifteen, especially among boys. In the 1990 survey figures for girls were lower; 43 per cent of fourteen and fifteen-year-olds masturbated and later this rose to 62 per cent. Girls were rather more inhibited. Is that still the case in 2010? Probably not.

A survey from 2008 showed that over 90 per cent of women between the ages of 18 and 30 masturbated and that two-thirds did so three times a week. Obviously great changes are taking place, since in 1979 the percentage that masturbated was 74 per cent and in 1953 only 62 per cent.

In the 1990s a young people's magazine conducted a survey on masturbation among young people. On average female readers of *Yes* started masturbating at the age of thirteen. The survey produced some remarkable statistics. On feelings of shame, for example: 63 per cent of (mainly young) women were somehow embarrassed to talk about masturbation. This aspect was mentioned in the introduction. 'Of girls claiming that they had achieved orgasm,' the magazine reported, '71% masturbate, while of girls claiming never to have achieved orgasm, only 35% do so.'

A survey among readers of a women's magazine found that 58 per cent engaged in masturbation. The average age of this group was certainly higher than that of female readers of the young people's magazine.

Men can find a similar questionnaire in an international survey conducted by *Playboy*. Forty per cent of respondents masturbated – 'operated the joystick', to use a popular transatlantic euphemism – more than once a week. But the same group of men hastened to add that they made love at least as often. In so doing they unintentionally underline the taboo. Because who wants to be a sad jerk-off?

Despite all the progress, at least in terms of numbers, there are still people who see the area as a business opportunity. In February 2009 a Flemish daily carried the headline 'Partners Cash in on Masturbating Girls'. The report was as follows:

> Two young Belgian businessmen have hit the jackpot thanks to their internet hype campaign among girls: *We Masturbate (Yes We Do)*. The smart entrepreneurs have marketed stickers and T-shirts bearing their logo, which are hugely popular with hip teenagers. According to Toon Carpentier (23) and Bert Dries (19) masturbation is nothing to be ashamed of. The two

Limburg-based students of physics and graphic design want use the *We Masturbate* logo to break the taboo surrounding masturbating girls. 'With boys masturbation is much more accepted. With games like 'willy-pulling' they virtually grow up with it. With girls there is much more of a taboo. By using modern means of communication in our own refreshing way, we're putting the item on the agenda,' says Carpentier. In addition they see their aim as a fusion between youthful creativity and entrepreneurial flair.

Using social networking sites like Netlog and Facebook, over twenty thousand teenage girls have joined the *We Masturbate (Yes We Do)* group.

Based on the many changes in the sexual field in recent decades, people assume that masturbation is generally no longer a problem. However, large-scale surveys among young people of upbringing, sexuality and early childhood experiences indicate that slightly less than half of them (sixteen-year-olds and below) still sometimes worry about it. Analysis of sections of interviews showed that worries fall into four categories: guilt feelings, fear of disease, fear of and embarrassment about being discovered and doubts and uncertainty caused by ignorance. These categories can be easily traced back to the myths about masturbation that have existed since time immemorial. All despite the knowledge that (oversimplifying) there is more and more solitary sex about. Who could have imagined thirty years ago that the sexual revolution would implode into mass masturbation in front of one's own computer? How many parents block internet sites showing porn? Is the subject discussed?

Only forty years ago many boys were definitely taken to task about it, especially if their mother had trouble getting the sheets clean.

How many parents, themselves children of the sexual revolution, prepare their own sons or daughters, in an easy-going way of course, for what awaits them in puberty? Perhaps that might prevent a few guilt feelings. Why not simply tell them that masturbation is a 'normal' activity? It has even been documented in male foetuses, or at least the Israeli gynaecologist Meizner, while carrying out an ultrasound examination of a pregnant uterus, observed a foetus of approximately 28 weeks making repetitive movements of its penis with its hand. In Meizner's view it looked very much like masturbation. The ultrasound images accompanying his article on the subject in a medical journal are very convincing.

Even medical students worry about masturbation. Every academic year at the university where I work an anonymous survey on sex is conducted, and what do we find, after all these years? In 2009 almost 20 per cent of both male and female trainee doctors felt guilty after masturbating and 2 per cent of women also felt lonely. Among male doctors-to-be feelings of loneliness are experienced by almost 10 per cent!

Adults and the elderly, fat and thin

Recent surveys indicate that almost all men masturbate, at all ages, even when they are in a relationship. The percentage of women who masturbate is lower than that of men. Many women still feel embarrassed when asked about masturbation and the suspicion is consequently that a considerable proportion still answer incorrectly in the negative. And then there is the fact that, in comparison with men, women have the great advantage that for them masturbation causes no mess and usually leaves no visible trace.

Erring on the side of caution, researchers assume that between 70 per cent and 80 per cent of adult women masturbate with some regularity. In fact, for many women it is their only means of achieving orgasm. Of course masturbation can provide a solution when one partner's sexual needs are greater than the other's. Subsequently guilt may rear its head, and the idea may take hold that

by masturbating you are withholding something from your partner, that you are 'playing away with yourself'. As a result it often
happens in secret.

Figures are also available for the middle-aged and the elderly.
In 2004 the American Association of Retired Persons (AARP) sur-
veyed 1683 people aged 45 and over. It was found that of women
in the age range 45–50 almost half still masturbated, while 20 per
cent of women aged 70 and above were still active (Jacoby 2005).
A majority of older women considered masturbation an important part of their sex lives, whatever their age.

Every urologist knows that elderly men masturbate. Patients
with superficial bladder tumours attend regularly to have their
bladders monitored and to produce urine samples to check for the
presence of malignant cells. It is by no means uncommon for the
pathologist examining the urine under the microscope to see
sperm cells. The urologist then draws his or her own conclusion,
though without any judgemental comment, such as 'dirty old
man', etcetera.

Generally speaking, the figures on the frequency of masturbation are lower in scientific surveys than in reader surveys. This
is related to anonymity: when people are questioned without
anonymity, they tend to give socially desirable answers. Women,
for example, are unlikely to say that they masturbate every day.

There are also differences between fat and thin people. Fat
people tend to masturbate more often in relative terms. This was
investigated by the Scottish psychologist Stuart Brody. Why is this?
Probably because they are less sexually attractive and hence have
more difficulty in finding a partner – as simple as that. Brody also
observed that intercourse is more effective than masturbation for
women wishing to keep their blood pressure low. He lists a number of reasons for this, including the fact that more areas of the
brain are active in coitus than in masturbation. In the vast majority of cases only the clitoris is stimulated, and not the vagina or
the neck of the womb. In Brody's view this does not produce a

'complete' orgasm, since the sensory nerves in the vagina are not stimulated. This means that no *oxytocin*, a hormone that produces contractions in the womb during orgasm, is released, resulting in a less satisfying climax. Brody is a psychologist attached to the University of Paisley in Scotland with a long list of publications to his name, but his central thesis is familiar: female orgasm through intercourse is superior to that obtained through masturbation – a very Freudian view. Later we will devote more attention to Brody's scientific work on hormones and orgasm.

In a society with high divorce rates, many men and women find themselves left to their own devices. Masturbation can help here too.

Times and locations

There are no statistics for the times at which people masturbate. Most probably it happens mainly just after waking and just before going to sleep, but increasingly men do it at their laptops, which is not very comfortable in bed. Obviously certain individuals will have particular preferences.

As with the preferred place of pleasure, there is no reliable data on how arousal is achieved in masturbation. In 2006 the online magazine Singlesite.nl conducted a survey among almost a thousand of its visitors. All of them turned out to indulge in 'do-it-yourself sex'; the survey showed that 42 per cent used mainly their own imagination, and in second place came the internet with 30 per cent. Non-online porn films did badly (6 per cent) and telephone sex lines were completely out of it: only 1 per cent were aroused by panting men and women on the other end of the line. As regards location (sitting at one's laptop was left out of account), almost half preferred to do it lying in bed, while the next most popular choices were the bath and the shower (14 per cent). The toilet did not prove popular, scoring only 3 per cent. Things are different at work. On 9 December 2009 it was reported that over

50 per cent of women masturbated at work, shown by a survey conducted by the Danish newspaper *Ekstra Bladet*. Men came off no better: 60 per cent admitted having sometimes masturbated in the boss's time. The toilet was favourite with both sexes. A Swedish newspaper had conducted a similar survey and its figures tallied quite closely with the Danish. When asked about it, the editor-in-chief of the Swedish paper said: 'One person smokes, another masturbates, and provided it doesn't harm the environment, it's all right by me.'

As far as I know a similar survey has never been carried out in the Netherlands. According to the writer Arnon Grunberg (1971–) the most popular place among military personnel stationed in Afghanistan is the shower, which should consequently not be entered without flip-flops – Grunberg describes the floor as slippery with sperm.

3

Education

How can a new generation of educators best deal with the topic of masturbation? How can we dispense with the need for refresher courses? Parents talk too little to their children about sexual desire and the emotional aspects of sex – and concentrate exclusively on the biological and technical aspects. 'The problem is', say the researchers, 'that sex education is mainly left to mothers. They find it difficult enough to instruct their daughters – being anxious to keep their own sex lives out of the picture – let alone their sons.'

According to the authors mothers find it embarrassing to talk about masturbation, ejaculations and the maturing of their children's genitals, so this is left to the fathers, who often shirk the task. Actually it is very simple: men don't talk about sex. They do talk about the trophy cabinet, about results and silverware, but not about the heart of the matter.

Loving yourself

Many children's libraries will have sex education books on masturbation. One booklet from 1999 contains such comments as 'there's absolutely nothing odd about having sexual feelings', 'playing with yourself is loving yourself' and 'you're the only person who's always there and available for sex when you feel like it'. A little further on we read: 'Sex is like snacking, you mustn't overdo it'. Under the heading 'addicted to sex' the author warns children to learn self-control, 'because you can become addicted to masturbation' and 'once you've learned self-control, you won't pester other people with your sexual urges'.

Boys are advised to ejaculate in a condom, a tissue or a handkerchief. 'If you masturbate at home, for instance, it's a nuisance for your mother, your little brother or your granny to see traces of sperm in the toilet or the bathroom.' Appropriately, that particular chapter is entitled 'Clean up the mess!' Girls who use their fingers to masturbate, and especially those who 'put something inside' are advised to clean everything thoroughly in order to avoid infection.

In an older sex education book from 1992, a number of awkward tips are given on, for instance, examining one's genitalia in the window of the oven or the television screen – presenting quite a challenge, especially to girls! Warnings are also dispensed. 'You mustn't put anything into your vagina that you wouldn't put into your mouth', or slightly further on: 'don't stick your willy into a vacuum cleaner hose'. Those warnings once persuaded me to acquire the book for our four children, three boys and a girl. The author calls masturbation a way of spoiling yourself: 'Like toasting a slice of white bread until it's honey-coloured, then spreading it with peanut butter and sprinkling chocolate on top. Lots of chocolate. And not wolfing it down, but cutting it into nice slices, like a cake, and then savouring it slowly.'

Unfortunately the role of fantasies is not given sufficient prominence in these publications. The extensive attention given to the physical side of masturbation contrasts with the cursory and generalized treatment of fantasies. A general explanation is followed by a number of exercises for boys who can't make it – meaning they can't 'come'. Fortunately you don't have to, but 'should you want to there are a number of things you can try, such as being good to yourself, learning to relax and acquiring sexual experience.'

All in all these are not books to give to children as standard when they leave primary school. Most twelve and thirteen-year-olds are not particularly keen on intimate questions and remarks on masturbation!

Nowadays parents can of course make use of the internet for their children's sex education. Useful sites include that of the Family Planning Association, www.fpa.org.uk, and www.children first.nhs.uk. Online sources can also advise on sex education literature from the bewildering variety available, for instance, at www.amazon.co.uk. Men can find a wealth of information on masturbation at www.jackinworld.com. I'm fairly sure that they can also manage to find www.pornotube.com without any help; www.doctorg.com/FemaleEjaculation is a particularly instructive site for adult women. YouTube has over 28,000 videos featuring masturbation.

Like adults, children sometimes use toys for masturbating. One example was more or less borrowed from Harry Potter. A few years ago the manufacturer Mattel, quite naively, introduced the 'Harry Potter Broomstick', a battery-powered toy resembling the 'flying Nimbus 2000 broom' in the films. The broom's special effects were that it made flying noises, and also vibrated. After the broom had been on the market for a while, some parents became

Nimbus 2000 Broom.

concerned when they found that young girls in particular seemed very fond of the toy.

A letter from a purchaser from Ohio read as follows:

When my twelve-year-old daughter asked for this broom for her birthday, I thought she was too old for it. But she's really crazy about it, and her friends like it too. They play with it for hours in the bedroom. What they like most are the special effects, the sounds and the vibrations.

It wasn't long before the toy was taken off the market.

Back in 1925

Every older reader has heard of thorny sex education books that afflicted the lives of his or her parents and grandparents: *Keeping Yourself Pure, The Doctrine of Chastity, Warning from a Friend of Young People, Treatise on the Characteristics, Causes, Hazards, Prevention, and Cure of Onanism or Self-Pollution*. The year 1925 saw the publication of a book, 136 pages long, called *Harmful or Harmless? New Insights on an Old Sexual Question*. The author, Pieter Johannes Smink (1885–1946), a devout Christian who had previously published some unremarkable pastoral books, used the elegant pseudonym A. Morvincit (Love Triumphs). It is typical of the time that the word onanism – 'masturbation' was not used at this time – does not occur anywhere in the prospectus. 'This work aims to give calm and liberating advice to those unreconciled to their own sexual urges who shun the solitary satisfaction of those urges as harmful or shameful.' This is the sort of language used. Probably only a few people benefited from the book, since it was confiscated soon after publication: it appeared several decades before its time.

In his introduction the writer set out his aim in writing the book:

There are thousands of people who live with their sexual urges as an animal tamer lives with his tigers; he does his best, but there's not much room in the cage, and he's only human, and the animals are unpredictable. The provisional aim of these pages is simply to contrast the simplicity of the sexual urge and the simplicity of its demands with the artificial way in which so many people confront that urge – or posture in the face of it. Against pomposity and posturing we set the voice that simply says 'yes' to life. That 'yes' accepts the sexual act as a means of expression, the expression as something liberating and liberation as a necessity. And where that expression cannot always – and sometimes does not want to – extend to intercourse, and in its solitude it is in any case a moment in the oneness of being, we wish in these pages to show how broad and rich the significance of the solitary sexual act can be.

This is plain speaking. A. Morvincit does not mince his words, but uses the word 'rich', which signals that this is not a moralist talking, but a generous spirit, who does his work seriously with a broad grin on his face.

Love Triumphs: 'The time is still far off when the plain names for sexual things will resonate with something of the divine power with which those things are imbued.'

Subsequently the writer clarifies some other words: *chiromania* (using the hand for sexual gratification) and *ipsation* (self-induced sexual excitement). The latter expresses clearly the fact that this is something someone does to themselves.

The writer commends popular terms, since in his view they name the act in an innocent way, without deprecation and with occasional good-natured humour. 'When Baden Powell states that boys among themselves refer to "bestiality", I believe that he is making a colossal mistake: denouncing one's natural urges is the exclusive prerogative of grown-ups.'

In his book Morvincit deals extensively with the work of such scientific authorities as Magnus Hirschfeld, Hermann Rohleder and Wilhelm Stekel. He quotes a case of the last of these – one of the few acolytes of Freud who regarded masturbation as a completely normal phenomenon – in order to demonstrate that penetrating a ewe with the penis is not strictly speaking masturbation, but that on the other hand a woman's achieving orgasm with the aid of flies *was*:

> Miss K.H. has taken to the following form of onanism, which gives her the most intense orgasm. On warm summer days she lies naked on the sofa, spreads her thighs and smears her vulva with honey. This attracts all the flies in the room and the tickling sensation of their feet on her vulva soon brings her to orgasm. She maintains that no other kind of auto-eroticism or sexual intercourse can produce an orgasm of such intensity.

Each of the previously mentioned well-known authorities, says Morvincit, reinvented the wheel in his own way: in his extensive works Magnus Hirschfeld (1868–1935), one of the founders of sexology, identifies *onania prolongata*, in which manual stimulation is discontinued whenever a climax is approached and shortly after resumed. In Hirschfeld's view *Onania interrupta*, that is, without orgasm, is more common than is assumed. It is usually practised by 'young men who believe that they will avoid the dreaded harmful consequences as long as they ensure that no seed leaves their bodies'. Finally there is *onania incompleta*, in which sexual satisfaction is achieved but without ejaculation, an improbable combination. It does occur, though, but really only in preadolescent boys.

The greatest sexual reformer, Sigmund Freud (1856–1939), classified masturbation by age: infantile masturbation, by which he means all auto-erotic acts that lead to sexual satisfaction, child masturbation and adolescent masturbation.

A. Morvincit continues:

> Life, and every urge, expresses itself in diversity. Life is a wondrous spring of ever-new kinds of desire. We saw from the diversity of masturbation how people strive in manifold ways to reach their source of pleasure and manage to refresh themselves at that source. The universality and unconditionality of that striving will become clear as we move on to consider the widespread nature of masturbation.

This research might strike us as naive – whoever researches the spread of love? – were it not for the fact that this liberal Christian writer (who belongs to the Dutch Reformed Church, for those still familiar with such things) was bold enough to dismiss wrong-headed exhortations and warnings directed at masturbators and hence to liberate them from the oppressive and humiliating delusion that they are the only one.

'People must learn to love themselves and to find an object outside themselves, to understand the cosmic sense of sexual desire in sexual congress with the one they love and are loved by. But you *begin* with yourself and no one else.'

Masturbation after circumcision

As far as I know it has never been scientifically investigated, but it seems that as puberty approaches boys learn about masturbation more easily than girls. An additional advantage for boys is that in puberty the adhesion between the inner and outer foreskin are released. Some mothers are inclined to break such adhesions at an earlier age by forcibly stripping the foreskin from the head of the penis. Generally speaking this is not a good idea.

While we are talking about the foreskin: does it matter when it comes to masturbation whether a man or a woman is circumcised or not? Almost all uncircumcised men masturbate by moving their foreskin over the head of their penis. So there is nothing strange about a man considering circumcision wondering what it will be like without a foreskin. Sometimes people are frightened masturbation will not be possible at all after circumcision. This is a common misunderstanding. It may occasionally happen that a circumcised man needs a lubricant (or saliva, oil or even shampoo, although the latter is not advisable) because circumcision has been so tight that no movement is left in the remaining skin during an erection.

Fortunately most men are circumcised in the correct way and hence there is enough play in the skin. Masturbation proceeds in exactly the same way as with uncircumcised men. The only difference is that most circumcised men hold their penis slightly lower down, below the head, and move the skin there up and down. After circumcision the skin can no longer be moved back and forth over the head, but that makes no difference to a circumcised man's enjoyment of masturbation. When he masturbates, he usually automatically also rubs the edge, the underside or other parts of the head, which in this way receives direct stimulation.

In the initial period after circumcision the skin may feel rather tight, and a lubricant may be necessary, but after between two and six months the skin will automatically become suppler with practice and there will be a greater range of movement. It is important not to try to force things, otherwise too much tension will be exerted on the place where the stitches were previously located. An alternative method of masturbation for circumcised men is to lie supine and run the penis over a cushion or a mattress.

Very little information is available about masturbation by circumcised women. Only in the most extensive form of circumcision in girls is the clitoris largely removed. This procedure is called *infibulation*, and in Africa 15 per cent of all female circumcisions are carried out in this way. In such a case in a man, this would be called partial amputation of the penis. The remains of the labia majora are then stitched together, leaving a small aperture for menstruation and urination. Masturbation has been rendered impossible, or so one would think. However, in the scientific literature there are reports that radically circumcised women, certainly after defibulation, the re-opening of the access to the vagina, can still reach orgasm, though mainly vaginal.

In some traditions ritual circumcision is carried out by simply holding a knife against the vagina, or some hair is shaved off or the clitoris is pierced. Activists are campaigning for such ritual circumcision to be offered as an alternative.

The form of circumcision, the age at which it is carried out and the method used depend on the circumstances: the ethnic background, the country or region, urban or rural location and socio-economic status. The operation can be performed at different ages, varying from shortly after birth to the period of the first pregnancy. It is usually carried out on girls aged between four and eight. According to the World Health Organization the age is falling, indicating that circumcision is less and less linked to rites marking initiation into adulthood and full membership of the clan.

Some undergo the operation alone, but generally girls are circumcised in groups, often of sisters or neighbours. The procedure may be performed at home, at a neighbour's house, in a clinic or at a specially chosen location. The latter is usually the case with initiation rites, for which a sacred tree or river is chosen. The circumcision may be carried out by an older woman, a traditional midwife or shaman, a barber or a qualified doctor or midwife. The girls are sometimes aware of what is about to happen and sometimes not. The ritual is frequently accompanied by festivities and presents. In the case of initiation rites it is a festive occasion for the whole community.

The Female Circumcision Act of 2004 made the practice illegal in the UK and similar legislation exists in most EU states.

Masturbation and the mentally handicapped

Some men and women are completely unable to masturbate. These are not people suffering from a double wrist fracture – a quite rare occurrence – but mainly men, women and children with a mental handicap, who require assistance when sexually aroused.

On this subject my attention was caught by an internet report of March 2009 under the heading 'Nurses Forced to Masturbate'. What had happened? In New Zealand an investigation had been instituted after six nurses had complained at being required to assist mentally handicapped patients in masturbating. The facility where the women worked, New Zealand Care, denied the imputations, but according to the *Nelson Evening Mail* did admit that it had launched an inquiry into the matter after five of the six women had resigned. The affair was even discussed in parliament.

MP Nick Smith submitted an official complaint to the Minister of Health and demanded an in-depth inquiry. 'These accusations are so appalling as to be scarcely credible, but the nurses strike me as sincere, honest and very credible,' said the MP. One of the nurses said that the task of helping patients achieve sexual satisfaction had been raised during training sessions. Another said: 'Masturbation was a topic at virtually all sessions.' According to a spokesperson for the hospital the topic of 'intimacy with patients' had indeed been broached during courses, but concerned nothing beyond the washing of patients.

This is a tricky subject in healthcare. I know from personal observation in the 1970s as a third-year medical student in what was then still called a lunatic asylum that on occasion some nurses helped patients achieve sexual satisfaction. It was also openly discussed. I have unfortunately not been able to obtain information about the current state of affairs, because of the taboo on the subject.

At the other end of the spectrum is a small group of mentally handicapped individuals who masturbate excessively and do not observe the usual norms of decent behaviour. In many cases these are autistic children, who masturbate compulsively in public. Often it is the parents who sound the alarm. If a behavioural approach does not help, the usual alternative is treatment with a medication like mirtazapine, which is generally used as an anti-depressant, or with a so-called antiandrogen, which almost always solves the problem. The anti-androgen drug cyproterone acetate (Androcur®) is the most frequently prescribed. Excessive masturbation may also be found in men with Parkinson's disease as a result of the medication they have to take. This can be very expensive for the men affected, especially if it is combined with visits to sometimes costly porn sites. Hypersexuality, the technical medical term, is often accompanied by an excessive urge to gamble.

Masturbation to order

When there are problems of conception, artificial insemination is sometimes an option. In this process sperm cells are injected into the woman at the appropriate moment in order to increase the chance of pregnancy. Couples are eligible for this treatment if the husband's sperm is of poor quality, if antibodies to sperm are present in the cervical mucus or in the case of unexplained infertility. Three types of insemination are possible.

The least invasive technique is AIH (artificial insemination with the husband's sperm). In this case the sperm is inserted high in the vagina close to the cervix. With IUI (intrauterine insemination) the sperm is inserted beyond the cervix in the womb itself. In some hospitals the term 'artificial insemination' is used for both insemination techniques, despite the difference between them. With both AIH and IUI the man produces sperm through masturbation in the so-called 'gentlemen's room' or 'sperm room' of the fertility clinic. In the United States the gentlemen's room is also sometimes called the 'masturbatorium'. The sperm is then processed in the laboratory and the liveliest spermatozoa are selected using a kind of centrifuge.

In practice, the process of producing sperm in the gentlemen's room does not always prove successful, in other words, masturbating on demand in strange surroundings is far from a sinecure for many men. Many sperm donors literally and figuratively clam up, and some men have objections of principle, though for these there are fortunately special sperm-friendly condoms with which sperm can be collected via sexual intercourse.

In the case of an ordinary sperm check, for example after sterilization, the sperm can be ejaculated at home. The man must not have had an ejaculation for between three and five days before submission of a sample, which must be taken to the hospital in the appropriate jar within two hours. The sperm sample must be carried on the person's body, for example in a trouser pocket, to prevent cooling.

Workshops for women: lessons in masturbation

It is clear from Eve Ensler's episodic play *The Vagina Monologues* of 1996 that many women have no idea what their genitals look like. If they are asked to describe or draw their vagina they produce very odd impressions. A pregnant woman drew a huge bawling mouth with coins falling out of it, another, thin woman, a large tray with a cream cake on it. Yet another imagined a kind of anatomical vacuum, through which moisture from the environment occasionally trickles. This is more or less comparable with the representation by Leonardo da Vinci (1452–1519) of the vagina as a great gaping hole. The great man was gay, which may have played a role. In 1476 he was arrested on suspicion of sodomy with a male prostitute called Jacopo Saltarelli. Several historians are convinced that through the intercession of the Tornabuoni family he was released after two hearings. His drawing of a vulva is owned by Queen Elizabeth II and is kept at Windsor Castle.

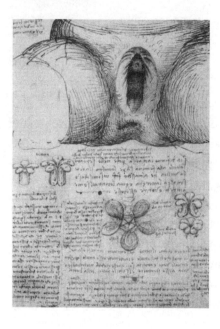

Leonardo da Vinci, *Vulva*, 1504–9.

As long ago as the 1950s American researcher Alfred Kinsey found that the way in which most women had become acquainted with sex before marriage was not as important as the question whether or not they had achieved orgasm during their pre-marital experiences. Women who had proved capable of orgasm by any means before marriage responded to sex in their marriage with an orgasm three times as frequently as those who had never previously experienced one.

Masters and Johnson found in their research for their book *Human Sexual Response* that an orgasm achieved through masturbation was reached more quickly and was generally more intense than one produced by a partner.

The reason why masturbation is normally an excellent way of achieving orgasm is that no one can distract the man or woman masturbating. He or she can concentrate entirely on themselves and take as long over it as necessary. But we have to learn how to do it properly, a point made by the poet Adriaan Morriën (1912–2002) in 'The Use of a Wall Mirror':

Home alone, naked on my bed,
I hold the mirror from my parents' room
right over me and support it with my left hand,
while I masturbate with my right.

I look at the reflection of my pasty skin,
my skinny arms, lanky legs,
my suntanned face, still boyish, spectacled.

Only half in love with myself
I try to discern myself
as a mirror image and fellow-lover –
I'd rather be in a girl's arms.

My eyes are trained on me: I'm not ashamed.
There's no cause to fathom my look.

I listen to the silence of the house,
the only one I trust.

Words are formed, as in someone fleeing in panic,
disjointed, unforgettable.

The effort it takes to keep the mirror still
and not to let the right hand's movement
slacken: a rhythmic beat
I must keep firmly in hand,
practised home alone on other afternoons,
or at bedtime
while thinking of a girl,
or rather a score of girls
whom I wedded in a trice.

Pianists are made, not born.

Whatever has become twisted in someone's childhood through feelings of shame and guilt can gradually be straightened out in a reasoned way, if necessarily rigorously. For example, decades ago the writer and psychologist Yvonne Kroonenberg found herself at a masturbation weekend in Amsterdam, led by the American sexologist Betty Dodson. 'A curious person,' wrote Kroonenberg, 'short, stocky, somewhere in her early sixties.' In Dodson's view masturbation is the basis of all sex: you must first get to know yourself before you can enjoy it with other people. And learn to love yourself (where have we heard that before?). She seemed to be talking sense. Yvonne tells the story:

> Thirteen women in a circle, each with their own story: one who's never been able to come, two caught in the act as children, a Tantra fan, all naked from the waist down and with their legs apart. I must admit that I've never before been able to look other people's private parts with so little embarrassment. The exercises were not all easy to understand – it began with a breathing exercise with a finger in your nose. Nor were they all a turn on: the part with the thirteen cucumbers, for instance – participants first had to trim them to their ideal size.
>
> It was instructive, though. We also learned about the social and psychological background to masturbation, about upbringing, guilt feelings, about orgasm and the location of the G spot. No room for embarrassment, no faking orgasm, no having to hold back orgasm. Especially not the latter – from her case Ms Dodson produced some impressive dildos, which no one could resist. Except for the one woman who had never come, that is.

The Vagina Monologues also contains a report of a masturbation workshop. The women were asked to examine their vagina carefully and extensively with a hand mirror and then tell the group what they saw. One participant says that up to that point everything she knew about her vagina she had on hearsay or had made up herself. She had never seen her vagina and it had never occurred to her to take a look at it. These are her words:

> It seemed so reductive and awkward to look at it, getting down there the way we did in the workshop, on our shiny blue mats, with our hand mirrors. It reminded me of how the early astronomers must have felt with their primitive telescopes.
>
> I found it quite unsettling at first, my vagina. Like the first time you see a fish cut open and you discover this other bloody complex world inside, right under the skin. I was so raw, so red, so fresh. And the thing that surprised me most was all the layers. Layers inside layers, opening into more layers.

The participant was deeply impressed by her vagina. She had discovered El Dorado! All she wanted was to lie on a mat with her legs apart and explore her vagina for ever more. It was more beautiful than the Grand Canyon and at the same time it had the fresh innocence of a neat English garden. When the workshop leader asked who had ever had an orgasm, only two women put their hand up. The narrator did not raise her hand. Orgasms had happened to her, for example, in her dreams. She often had them in water, on horseback or on a vaulting horse at the gym. She *had* had orgasms, but she didn't know how! Climaxing had something mystical about it for her, and nothing must interfere with it. Trying to force things oneself didn't 'feel right'. It was so phoney . . . The element of surprise would be lost. The basic problem was that those unforced orgasms had not happened for quite a while, and that was the reason she was taking part in the workshop. Then came the moment she had been hoping for, but had also dreaded. They had to search for their clitoris:

> We were there, the group of us women, on our backs, on our mats, finding our spots, our locus, our reason, and I don't

know why, but I started crying. Maybe it was sheer embarrassment. Maybe it was knowing that I had to give up the fantasy, the enormous life-consuming fantasy, that someone was going to do this for me – the fantasy that someone was coming to lead my life, to choose direction, to give me orgasms . . . I could feel the panic coming. The simultaneous terror and realization that I had avoided finding my clitoris, had rationalized it as mainstream and consumerist because I was in fact terrified that I did not *have* a clitoris . . . The woman who ran the workshop saw my insane scrambling, sweating, and heavy breathing. She came over. I told her, 'I've lost my clitoris. It's gone. I shouldn't have worn it swimming.'

The woman leading the workshop had to laugh. She calmly stroked the narrator's forehead. She said 'you can't lose your clitoris just like that'. The clitoris was here, the door bell of her house, and her house itself. The session continued:

I lay back and closed my eyes. I put the mirror down. I watched myself float above myself. I watched as I slowly began to approach myself and reenter. I felt like an astronaut reentering the atmosphere of the earth. It was very quiet, this reentry: quiet and gentle. I bounced and landed, landed and bounced. I came into my own muscles and blood and cells and then I just slid into my vagina. It was suddenly easy and I fit. I was all warm and pulsing and ready and young and alive. And then, without looking, with my eyes still closed, I put my finger on what had suddenly become me. There was a little quivering at first, which urged me to stay. Then the quivering became a quake, an eruption, the layers dividing and sub-dividing. The quaking broke open into an ancient horizon of light and silence, which opened onto a plane of music and colors and innocence and longing, and I felt connection calling connection as I lay there thrashing about on my little blue mat.

Betty Dodson is almost certainly correct in saying that a masturbation course is the best and easiest way of discovering how to reach orgasm and what method of stimulation is the most effective. In that way, she believes, you are also better equipped to help your partner achieve sexual satisfaction. There is, though, a dangerous pattern of reasoning behind this. Isn't it a covert variation on the age-old theme of man's oppression of woman? Much literature in praise of masturbation seems to work on the assumption that the woman's genitalia are a kind of domestic appliance whose owner has not understood the directions properly, so that an 'expert' is required to explain to women how their sex organs are constructed and how optimum operation can be achieved.

Betty Dodson wrote a book on her virtually lifelong fight for masturbation under the title *Sex for One – the Joy of Self-Loving*, which first appeared in 1974 and was last reprinted in 1996. It makes for pretty dry reading! Only the tenth chapter on masturbation as a form of meditation is really interesting. See also www. bettydodson.com.

I once heard someone sigh that all the fuss about masturbation training can best be compared to the first time a woman bakes a cake. There is a good chance that it will stick to the cake tin or even burn. Fortunately most women persevere, that is they keep trying and even brave repeated failures. Until the result is really moreish!

The poet Bart Brey sees men as making the 'batter':

Masturbating, I plug
the cracks in the dikes.

I whip thick cream in the wind
and with it stop the fissures.

Or hurl it on the coast
of unrestrained desire.

To get back home at nights
first I must do my rounds.

I always find a reason
to take myself in hand.

To make a nice new batter.

Jamye Waxman, a protégée of Betty Dodson's, writes in *Getting Off: A Woman's Guide to Masturbation* (2007), in a refreshingly upbeat and matter-of-fact tone on the subject:

> Let's face it, masturbation has been around as long as there has been someone who had something that felt good to stroke or rub. Some still argue that masturbation is evil, more evil than the teacher who made you stay after school to scrape gum out from under the desks. Others believe that masturbation is healthy, like eating your fruits and steaming your vegetables.

Rachel Swift, in *Women's Pleasure, or How to Have an Orgasm as Often as You Want* (1993), sees masturbation as central to the project.

Multiple orgasms

'When a woman masturbates she can reach orgasm in as little as forty seconds, and achieve several subsequent orgasms,' writes Sheila Kitzinger in her book *Woman's Experience of Sex*, 'while making love with a partner it can take two hours'. That is, if the partner has not long since gone off to wash the car or eat a bowl of muesli.

In 1990 Veronique van Dijk wrote the following poem in the magazine *Parmentier* on women's ability to achieve multiple orgasms while masturbating:

The day begins, the windows fill with sun
I'm drowsy, languid and quite numb
Springs squeak as I stretch in my bower
Give me a moment: I just have to come

The paper boy is whistling on his run
The squeaking gate: the morning paper's come
I really ought to go and have a shower
Give me a moment: I just have to come

The dog's impatient for a romp and fun
And whines and scratches, indignant and dumb
'Just coming,' I shout and curse and get sour
Give me a moment: I just have to come

There's no stopping me now I've really begun
The bright morning light that's making me hum
Only adds to the mounting excitement's power
Give me a moment: I just have to come

The masturbation repertory

A girl's exploration usually starts by stroking the clitoris in various
ways and cautiously exerting pressure. What happens if I rub a little
harder? Some women prefer to stimulate the tip of the clitoris
directly, but often it is too sensitive. It is more pleasant to touch the
immediately adjacent areas. Many adult women rub up and down
over their clitoris with a finger, varying the speed and pressure.
Or the clitoris is held between the index and middle finger, so that
the up-and-down movement also stimulates the immediately
adjacent area. Let's be clear about it: a penis, however hard, can't
manage all this.

Of course a woman will develop her own favourite repertoire.
In her book *Women's Pleasure* Rachel Swift gives tips for beginners:

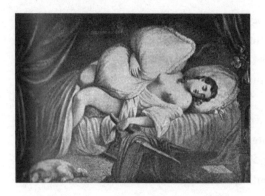

A. Borel, *Dream of Longing*, 19th-century lithograph.

Complete relaxation is essential. Make sure you will not be disturbed. Disconnect the phone, close the curtains, shut the doors – do whatever is necessary to put yourself at ease and make you confident that you won't be interrupted. Since this is your first time, allow yourself at least an hour during which you know you can be alone . . .

Put yourself to bed – alone, of course – and lie in a warm and comfortable position. If the thought of removing all your clothes makes you nervous, then leave some on.

Open your legs. Begin by exploring your body very gently with your hands, up and down your torso, over your breasts, in whichever way feels most enjoyable. Now bring your hands down between your legs. Gently explore all around the area of your genitals, probing and rubbing, in whichever manner pleases you most. You will probably find that one area is more sensitive than another and by using your fingers to manipulate it you can produce a pleasant sensation that seems to extend vaguely into other parts of your body. It is not the same as the pleasurable relief one derives from rubbing or scratching some other part of your body; it is warmer, making you slightly breathless and perhaps want to tense your legs, and it is much more directly *pleasurable* . . . Other women do active movements against things, for example putting a pillow between their legs . . .

That was popular in the past too, as can be seen in a nineteenth-century engraving.

Fingering

The practice just described is popularly known as 'fingering'. A Dutch cabaret song devoted to it was sung by Adèle Bloemendaal and by Nelleke Burg. It is called 'The Finger Song', but I came across another title, 'The Prince':

> His charm could not be greater
> And in bed he's just the tops
> Who is that Prince Charming
> Of whom each young girl dreams
>
> It's your finger
> Your own nice finger
> That's the prince of whom each young girl
> Dreams
>
> It doesn't stink of spirits
> Or dribble down your back
> It just does the business
> And doesn't ever slack
> Your body's labyrinthine
> But it knows the ins and outs
> And you can hide it quickly
> If Mum comes hereabouts.
>
> Imagine you're a queen
> And hubbie's away again
> Who's to help then
> When solitude's a strain

It's your finger
Your own dear finger
At least it has no mistress
In Paris

The world's a rotten place
There's not much love around
It's only your own finger
Will never let you down
Though they tell you it's not right
The Church's priests and lords
Are on their knees each night
Repolishing their swords

When girls say 'I don't want to'
They're not just playing coy
But it can take some time
Explaining to the boy

But I've never had to give
My finger, my own dear finger,
A good kick
In the balls

Lala . . .

Let's go far back in time to 1655, which saw the appearance of the celebrated anonymous French novel *L'Escole des filles* (Girls' Education). The book contains frank discussions of sex between a sixteen-year-old girl and her older, worldly wise cousin. It has splendid illustrations, and includes an impressive scene on the delights of masturbation. It concerns the daughter of a king who has a bronze statue made for her equipped with a phallus made of flexible material. The member was vertical and hollow and had a red tip with a small aperture in, with two appendages in the shape of testicles, all in faithful imitation of nature. Whenever the young lady's ardour was aroused by the manly figure she would rush to the statue and thrust it into her vagina, clasping the statue's buttocks and hugging it. Just before she reached her climax, she would press a spring on one of the buttocks, whereupon the statue propelled a warm, dense liquid, as thick as porridge, into her vagina, and so satisfied her.

Another leap in time to the recent past. In the 1970s Shere Hite (1942–) conducted a large-scale survey of the details of the sexual repertoire of American women at the time. With masturbation direct massaging of the clitoris (with the hand, a vibrator or a jet of hot water from a shower head) was seldom accompanied by vaginal, that is, penetrative stimulation, but there turned out to be a modest group who did not need to touch themselves at all. They could reach orgasm by rhythmically flexing the muscles in their pelvic floor and thighs. It is consequently no accident that in the nineteenth century cycling and horse-riding were considered unsuitable for young women. It was feared that their sexual feelings would ignite prematurely. The development of the treadle sewing machine also created considerable concern, particularly the type where two pedals had to be moved alternately. More of that anon.

Yet another group of women are able to achieve orgasm in relative calm at the hairdresser's. An example is found in the poem 'At the Hairdresser' by Anna Enquist (1945–):

Here is the chair. There in the silver,
a foundling so tired and trim,
a fleshly find has been placed.
He strokes the hypothetical hair;
his look rebounds to the reversed
space behind me where his gallant
gesture is received by black goldfish
that get things wrong.

Brush and broom. In vicious heels
they crack the curls of their mothers. Ivory-coloured
the wet and naked face above the
black cape. In the miniature
night my hand joylessly searches for
a sign of life, explores my sex
enquiring about the body lying there.

How the sharp metal starts
to gleam, the scissors, the razor;
how numbly with deadened eyes
I stare through the strange window – rain,
remnants of snow, afternoon light – .
How secretly, from the hip, I shoot
crystal lamps, mirrors into freed
shards. How they tinkle. How I tingle.

Long ago Dr Von Schrenck-Notzing reported cases of ladies who 'masturbated in response to sensual stimuli that had nothing to do with sex, for instance, on hearing music, on contemplating landscape paintings, on viewing splendid natural beauty, etc.'
So there really is nothing new under the sun!

The female prostate and ejaculation

Since 1880 the female prostate has been known as Skene's glands, after an American gynaecologist who at the end of the nineteenth century published an article on the female prostate. The glands should really have been named after Reinier de Graaf (1641–1673). At the end of his short life de Graaf made a study of this rudimentary organ. He also observed at that early date that women ejaculate. It may be relevant that many of his test subjects worked as prostitutes and could talk openly about the subject.

The man who made the female prostrate his life's work was Professor Milan Zaviačič. In 1999 he published a monograph entitled *The Human Female Prostate*. He was a professor of pathology in Bratislava, which is why the results of his research initially had scarcely any impact on urology, gynaecology and sexology. For decades there was only minimal contact between scientists from the West and those from the Eastern block.

It has been shown that the female prostate produces the same substances as the male, including a prostate-specific antigen (PSA), a marker substance used in screening men for prostate cancer. The rudimentary prostate is located between the vagina and the urethra. The drainage ducts issue into the urethra. It weighs approximately one tenth of a man's, that is, between 3 and 5 grams. In the majority of women the glandular tissue is concentrated beneath the end of the urethra.

At the beginning of his career particularly Milan Zaviačič did not have two cents to rub together, which meant that he had to keep his research simple. One brilliant brainwave was to have women walk around for four days in the same cotton panties and then apply specific colours to substances, including acid phosphatase, which occurs in high concentrations in male prostate fluid. In the exact spot where the end of the urethra had rested against the cotton, was the colour of acid photophase. The stains indicated prostate fluid. The proof had been found.

Several researchers have tried to establish the volume that women ejaculate. The quantities found varied from 3 to 50 millilitres per ejaculation. By no means all women experience an ejaculation as such. Estimates vary between 6 per cent and 40 per cent. Nevertheless it is very probable that a form of ejaculation takes place in all women. One way in which this was researched was to collect ejaculate and determine the PSA content. Of course one can also compare urine before and after orgasm. Post-orgasmic urine will normally be mixed with prostate fluid.

So what is the importance of the existence of a female prostate for gynaecology, urology and sexology? As regards sexology it is reasonable to assume that the Gräfenberg (or G) spot described in the last century is none other than the female prostate. It is also a place where many nerve-endings are found. For a urologist it is important to know that some 10 per cent of documented cases of cancer of the urethra relate to so-called adenocarcinomas, where the cancer originates in glandular tissue, in this case from the prostate gland. In addition it should be stressed that the female prostate can become inflamed and that for that reason a treatment with, for instance, nitrofurantoin in the case of inflammation of the urethra is not sufficient. This kind of drug only sterilizes the urine, but does not accumulate in prostate tissue.

The discovery of the clitoris

The novel *The Anatomist* by Argentine writer Federico Andahazi (1963–) appeared in 1997 in a translation by Alberto Manguel. This intriguing and enjoyable book is based on the life of the celebrated sixteenth-century Venetian anatomist Renaldus Columbus, who like his more illustrious namesake made a great discovery with far-reaching consequences. The novel revolves around his chance discovery of a previously uncharted area of the female body – the *kleitoris*.

Matteo Colombo is in love with the Venetian prostitute Mona Sofia. In an attempt to win her affections he experiments with aphrodisiac potions, which he tries out on a number of whores, unfortunately without the desired result.

Then one day Matteo Colombo is called to attend the beautiful but languishing widow Dona Ines. He examines her and to his astonishment sees a kind of penis, which although small, is incontrovertibly erect. When the mysterious organ is touched, Dona Ines is roused to unbridled passion. And so by accident Matteo hits upon the instrument with which he also hopes to win Maria Sofia's passion.

Title-page of Renaldus
Columbus, *Re Anatomica*
(1559).

But besides a lover Matteo Colombo is also a scientist and wants to publish his spectacular discovery. The Inquistion gets wind of this and forbids him to publicize his findings. For how calamitous it would be for Christianity if the devil were to take control of the female organ of sin! Matteo is doomed to be tried before the Inquisition . . .

It is a historical fact that in 1559 Renaldus Columbus wrote a scientific description of the clitoris far more realistic and reliable than those of his predecessors. The problem was that he was something of a braggart, which led to peevish comments by his younger contemporaries. In the novel the reaction of the Inquisition to this discovery that poses a threat to the faith is the driving force of the drama. In reality a hilarious parallel occurred when the writer was awarded Argentina's principal literary prize for his work, but the lady whose name the prize bore refused to meet him. The amount of the prize arrived by an anonymous draft.

In the presence of others

The vast majority of human beings prefer to masturbate in private, but there are exceptions. A journalist working in my home town, Rob Zijlstra, describes such an exception in his collection of stories *Courtroom 14* (Part II). They make not very cheerful reading, dealing as they do with incest, violence, manslaughter, murder, drugs, and with a man accused of having masturbated in front of children in a GP's waiting room. What had happened? The man, a cook from England, had made an appointment with his GP. When he entered the waiting room at about nine-thirty, a little girl was also sitting there, playing. The accused sat down to wait. After ten minutes the girl's mother came out of the consulting room and they went off home together by bike. The cook was the next patient. According to the charge, he had taken his penis out of his trousers in the waiting room and masturbated. On the bike journey home the girl had told her mother that the gentleman in the waiting room had done funny things. First he had scratched his willy and then he had taken it out of his trousers. And then the gentleman had gone up and down with his fist. No, he hadn't said anything. The mother, very upset, had reported the incident to the police.

Zijlstra's observations in the court are fairly bland:

> Why should a girl of five tell a story like that, with details that girls of five cannot possibly know about yet? The suspect Jamie tells the magistrate he doesn't know either. He does have his version of events, though. It was raining when he had to go to the doctor's. So he took off his coat in the waiting room, and then saw to his horror that his zip was broken and the leading edge was jammed at the bottom. He was embarrassed and simply had to zip up his trousers. So he had stuck one hand in his trousers and tried to pull up the zip with the other.

The magistrate: 'You weren't wearing any underpants. Why not?'

Jamie: 'That was the fashion at the time. It isn't anymore.'

Magistrate: 'You're fashion-conscious?'

Jamie: 'I'm wearing underpants now.'

The prosecutor speaks briefly and to the point, and says: 'If there's one place where we should feel safe, it's the doctor's waiting room. Karin's story has the ring of truth, and her behaviour – anxious, recurrence of bedwetting – is familiar from these kinds of sex offences. And his account is weird nonsense.'

The prosecutor asks for a three-month provisional sentence with a three-year probationary period and compulsory supervision during rehabilitation, but the judge acquits Jamie, since there are too many areas of doubt. Deficiencies in the police investigation, testimony by a five-year-old child, with no corroboration apart from the mother's and an accused who denies the charge.

An interpreter says to Jamie, who had lived in the Netherlands for almost ten years: 'Not guilty. Case closed.' Jamie gets up, while the dismayed mother looks on incredulously. There end the observations of the author.

Finally, after all the science and the sordid side of things, a few facts about sustainability for the connoisseur. Since 2006 there has been a regular masturbation marathon. In 2008, after San Francisco and London, Copenhagen was the venue for the 'Masturbate-a-thon'. The organizer, Pia Struck Madsen, wanted to break taboos surrounding sexuality. 'With this event I want to gather men and women from all over the world to discuss masturbation. Despite the emancipated society we live in, it remains a taboo. By offering pleasure, relaxation and a sexual voyage of discovery, I hope to change some of that.'

Participants were given the choice of three groups: women separate, men separate or all together. After an open discussion on masturbation they were allowed to get down to business. These were people who felt like jerking off or fingering themselves together! In 2011 the marathon was again held in San Francisco, but as far as I know the next venue has not yet been decided.

4
Sex Aids

My starting point in writing this chapter was a newspaper report about a vibrator disguised as a memory stick. One can start by dealing in baby clothes and end up launching an online business in erotic items. For Gaïd Ombre it was a logical step. The overworked businesswoman found her sex life was taking something of a back seat and that led indirectly to the setting up of Sweet Suite, a web outlet for stylish sex gadgets. Like the vibrator, which charged up through a USB connection and which at a cursory glance is like an ordinary memory stick. It can also be found as lipstick, a toothbrush or a powder brush! For further information see www.sweetsuite.nl.

Let us begin with the simplest masturbation aids, in particular for women. It may be necessary to apply a little oil: massage oil, palm oil, but any kind of vegetable oil is suitable. Under no circumstances use Vaseline, which is not soluble in water and may cause problems if it gets into the vagina or the opening of the urethra. Perfumed massage oil may give added stimulation, but be sure that the oil does not contain alcohol. So to moisten things down below use oil, spittle or vaginal secretions.

Sex toys

Sex is often described as an amorous game, and in order to play you need toys. In *Sex Toys* (2003), Gina Valente, Lilian Krikhaar and Rob Haenen give a complete overview of erotic toys, from the popular Tarzan to vibrating lipstick. There are toys for him, toys for her and a number of exciting games. To put readers of both sexes on the right track, the site is full of many positive customer reactions and handy tips from people who are intimately acquainted with the toys. These are replicas of genitalia, with or without a vibrating function, inflatable dolls, whips, edible underwear, nipple clips and much more besides; all designed for masturbating or intensifying/prolonging the sensation, alone or as a couple. Of course one's personal input remains important. The book is divided into four sections: for her, for him, for him and her, 'pleasure stuff' like tie-on penises, paint for body-painting and an erotic pack of cards. A separate page is devoted to each item featuring a colour photo, a description, directions for use, tips from an expert and often also the opinion of a generally enthusiastic user. In addition there are some technical facts, an indication of price and rating ('warm', 'hot', 'red hot!'). It is clear that the book is published in association with the Christine le Duc retail chain, from the preface, from various points in the text and from the address list of branches. For anyone looking to add a new dimension to his or her love life, the booklet offers a handy overview with a touch of humour. I personally found 'Sex Sculpture' the nicest. The accompanying Penis Copy Kit is a package containing everything you need to make a rubber mould of your own erect penis: a cock ring, a cylinder, printing material, rubber paste and instructions. A nice job for a rainy Sunday afternoon. You can fill the mould with plaster of Paris and make countless castings, which you can, for instance, put on the mantelpiece or attach to the wall of the bathroom. A great idea, for example, for military personnel, ship's captains or overseas dredgers.

In her book *Bonk* the American writer Mary Roach gives a hilarious account of her visit to a factory making sex toys. The manager says that all the staff have become 'immune', so that the toys no longer have any sexual charge and are regarded like a key chain or a bag.

Mary watches women painting the heads of enormous flesh-coloured penises red. Their careful movements are more or less comparable with those of a prostitute giving a hand-job. Meanwhile the ladies are chattering and laughing; they are mainly Catholic Latinas aged between thirty and forty. From the rear-view mirrors of their parked cars hang plastic roses and dolls representing the Virgin Mary. When asked, the women confess that they have not told their families about the precise nature of their job, though they have disclosed 'that they work with plastic'. That is particularly true of the women working in the department where hair is attached to the *mons Veneris* of inflatable dolls.

Dildos, vibrators and pins

A vibrator is an electrical device use to stimulate sexual responses. (An *industrial* device producing vibrations is known as a 'shaker'.) Figures published by a major producer of erotic equipment indicate that over a million vibrators are sold annually in the Netherlands, which strikes me as quite enough!

In contrast to the dildo – which was used for sexual pleasure back in antiquity – the vibrator did not become widely known until around 1900. When in the 1960s the taboos surrounding sex more or less disappeared and women's liberation was at its height, the vibrator became increasingly popular as a sex toy. One humorist christened it the 'electronic milkman'. Nowadays plenty of women who object to the technological computer-deep frozen-instant society we live in consign vibrators, along with frozen pizzas, the plethora of phoney Facebook friends and cybersex, to the rubbish heap.

The vibrations concerned are usually produced by the high-speed operation of a small electric motor inside the vibrator with a weight attached that is slightly off-axis, that is, eccentrically.

There are also vibrators that work through a coil. Generally, the electric motor works from batteries, but there are also vibrators that have a mains connection. Battery-powered models are, it is true, rather noisier than mains-powered, and some women find this a nuisance. Are they perhaps worried that others will hear what they are up to? For those interested there is a vibrator museum: www.vibratormuseum.com.

One last thing about those batteries. Not so long ago a very nice female acquaintance of mine sighed poetically: 'If my husband could screw the way he can chat, my vibrator's batteries wouldn't be flat.'

A dildo is an oblong object with a smooth surface, usually in the shape of a human penis. It has no vibrating motor. Over the centuries a wide variety of materials have been used, including jade, ivory, leather and (precious) metals. An ancient dildo made of resin-coated camel dung was found in Africa. In recent decades most of these materials have been ousted. Most dildos are made of PVC, silicon rubber, rubber, latex or glass.

There are also double-ended dildos on the market, which are used mainly by gay men and women for simultaneous stimulation. These models can, however, be used by a single woman to penetrate both anus and vagina simultaneously, in more or less the same way that Satan was thought to violate unsuspecting women in the Middle Ages.

The origin of the word dildo has never been conclusively explained. In 1992 this lack of clarity led to a full-blown polemical exchange in the Netherlands' most respected daily, *NRC Handelsblad*. It all began with a column by the writer and journalist Hans van Straten (1923–2004) examining the etymology of 'dildo', to which his attention had been drawn by a book (1944) by Marlies Philippa on Arabic words in Dutch. She wrote: 'The dildo as a sex toy for helping give women sexual satisfaction first crops up in Elizabethan English in the second half of the sixteenth century.' The reference is probably to *The Choise of Valentines – On the*

Merie Ballad of Nash his Dildo by the English poet Thomas Nash (1567–1601), which was written in the last year of his life. He describes how his member lets him down at the supreme moment, and grumpily admonishes his reluctant organ:

> My little dildo shall supply your kind,
> A youth that is as light as leaves in the wind;
> He bendeth not, nor foldeth any deal,
> But stands as stiff as he were made of steel.

There are various explanations of the name dildo. In order of increasing probability:

It is a corruption of *this will do.*

It derives from *diddle-o* (one of the meanings of *to diddle* is to fool and masturbate).

It comes from the Italian *diletto*, meaning delight.

Or from the English word *dally.*

Or from Spanish; in that language 'dildo' occurs as the name of a species of cactus with a soft, strong trunk and vertical spines.

The last of these explanations led to further squabbling in the pages of the venerable newspaper. In English there are two meanings of 'dildo(e)' – the artificial penis and the cactus of the Cereus species, which like most cacti comes from the Americas. The dildo as a sex aid is named after the phallus-shaped *Cephalocereus royenii.* After all, a candle (cereus) is one of the most easily accessible forms of dildo . . . In a major Spanish language dictionary, it says that in Puerto Rico dildo is a popular name for various cactuses. The dildo as a cactus, it argues, came from the Caribbean, after which the English gave it its present meaning.

In brief, the last word has not yet been spoken about the etymology of dildo!

History

The use of instruments for solitary sexual satisfaction is very ancient. The oldest known dildo is a 20-centimetre-long stone phallus found in Germany, some 30,000 years old. A dildo dating from this period was also found in France. The next oldest finds date from 4000 BC, a leap of over 20,000 years: they were discovered in Pakistan and are assumed to have been used in the worship of the god Shiva.

From 3000 BC onwards date paintings from ancient Egypt depicting dancing women wearing large phalluses for the god Osiris. There are also examples of this in ancient Babylonian sculpture. The British Museum's collection contains a vase that could not be more explicit. The museum of ancient Pompeii is also interesting in this respect. The oldest texts in which the dildo is mentioned derive from the Greeks, who called it *olisbos*. Dildos were used by both men and women, and vases and murals depict various sexual activities involving dildos. They also occur in plays and poems. The Greeks made them of stone, leather or wood with olive oil as a lubricant. Women whose husbands had to spend an extended period away from home were given a dildo to prevent or cure hysteria. One of the causes of hysteria (*hystera* = womb), the Greeks believed, was lack of sperm.

In China seven bronze dildos were found in a Han dynasty tomb from 200 BC. It is thought that they were used by concubines or aristocratic women. From the beginning of the first millennium to the Renaissance virtually no information is available. It is known that in the fifteenth century Chinese women used dildos of lacquered wood with a decorated surface. Lesbian couples were already using one-piece double dildos.

In the West in the sixteenth century the manufacture of dildos became an art form. Members of the aristocracy had dildos in silver, ivory or other precious materials. The first texts in Italian in which dildos are mentioned also date from this period.

In the seventeenth century the dildo frequently occurred in bawdy verses and risqué songs. The preferred material in those days was glass. These were hollow and could be easily filled with warm water or milk, and also known as *godemichés*. In that way not only could an ejaculation be simulated but the dildo could be brought up nicely to body temperature. For instance, Pietro Fortini, a sixteenth-century novelist from Siena, refers in his novella *Dei Novizi* to 'the glass full of warm water, used by nuns to quell the gnawing of the flesh and satisfy themselves as well as they can'. He adds that widows and other women not wishing to become pregnant also used them. Incidentally the glass was also sometimes filled with urine.

In his *Satires* (I, 3) John Marston (1573–1634) writes of the mores of Elizabethan England:

Shal Lucea scorn her husbands luke-warme bed
(Because her pleasure being hurried
In ioulting Coach, with glassie instrument,
Doth far exceede the Paphian blandishment . . . [coitus]

While the godemiché may have become much less a part of everyday life than the vibrator and the dildo, it does have the nicest etymology, deriving from Latin *gaude mihi* ('give me pleasure'). In his *Erotika Biblion* John Marston gave the names of a series of devices used at the time for masturbation. After sowing his wild oats, the author was ordained as a priest.

Godemiché used to simulate ejaculation.

The seventeenth-century French poet Claude le Petit took the idea of literary masturbation so seriously that instead of the sturdy book covers usual in his day he wanted a flexible cover for his own work, so that the book could also be used as a dildo. A poet far ahead of his time, he was beheaded at the age of 23 for his amoral writings!

John Wilmot, Earl of Rochester (1647–1680) a protégé of Charles II and a scathing, often bawdy satirist, portrayed memorably by Johnny Depp in the film *The Libertine* (2004), personified this sex toy as 'Signior Dildo' in a dramatic poem:

> You ladies of merry England
> Who have been to kiss the Duchess' hand,
> Pray, did you not lately observe in the show
> A noble Italian called Signior Dildo . . .
>
> Our dainty fine duchesses have got a trick
> To dote on a fool for the sake of his prick,
> The fops were undone did their graces but know
> The discretion and vigour of Signior Dildo.
>
> The Duchess of Modena, though she looks so high,
> With such a gallant is content to lie,
> And for fear that the English her secrets should know,
> For her gentleman usher took Signior Dildo.
>
> The Countess o'th' Cockpit (who knows not her name?
> She's famous in story for a killing dame),
> When all her old lovers forsake her, I trow,
> She'll then be contented with Signior Dildo . . .
>
> Tom Killigrew's wife, that Holland fine flower,
> At the sight of this signior did fart and belch sour,
> And her Dutch breeding the further to show,
> Says, 'Welcome to England, Mynheer van Dildo.'

He civilly came to the Cockpit one night,
And proferred his service to fair Madam Knight.
Quoth she, 'I intrigue with Captain Cazzo; [i.e., prick]
Your nose in my arse, good Signior Dildo . . .

A rabble of pricks who were welcome before,
Now find the porter denied them the door.
Maliciously waited his coming below
And inhumanly fell on Signior Dildo.

Nigh wearied out, the poor stranger did fly,
And along the Pall Mall they followed full cry;
The women concerned from every window
Cried, 'For heaven's sake, save Signior Dildo.'

The good Lady Sandys burst into a laughter
To see how the ballocks came wobbling after,
And had not their weight retarded the foe,
Indeed 't had gone hard with Signior Dildo.

Sex aids are not exclusive to human culture: Lothar Dittrich, ex-director of Hanover Zoo, observed a female chimpanzee who used a piece of wood to satisfy herself several times a day. Besides Dittrich's account there are at least four other articles in scientific journals in which zoologists report similar behaviour.

The vibrator as a medical instrument

Today the vibrator is regarded as an item for private enjoyment, but this was not always the case. The first vibrators – from about 1880 – were medical instruments for use in the consulting room. Give doctors a gadget and they will find a use for it . . . What did those nineteenth-century doctors do with them? In the nineteenth century there were countless, sometimes bizarre, methods of

Consulting room where
hysterical women were
brought to orgasm.

stimulating the sick body: water cures, massages, electrostatic
ozone treatment. Much to the surprise of the American Rachel
Maines, author of *Technology of Orgasm* (1999), genital massage
was added, for the treatment of hysteria. From childhood on
Maines was interested in things that no one else gave a second
thought to. She studied history as part of her doctoral research,
and began collecting material on crochet and knitting. She
planned to study the period 1830–1930 extremely thoroughly.
While studying countless magazines devoted to knitting, crochet-

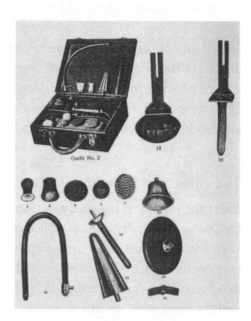

Set of vibrators
for medical use.

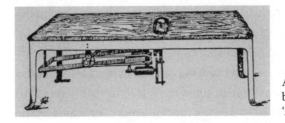

A treatment table with
built-in steam-driven
'Manipulator'.

ing and embroidery it struck her that there were a large number of
adverts for vibrators during that period. After completing her
thesis she was left with a thick folder full of clippings of these
adverts, and in this way was sucked into the world of medical
theories on the womb and hysteria.

Even in the oldest medical writings – those of Hippocrates
and Galen – there is mention of a cluster of ailments that have a
familiar ring today and even then were labelled 'hysteria'. Until
1900 it was thought that vague abdominal problems, dizziness,
insomnia, neurosis, epilepsy, mental deficiency and sexual apathy
all issued from problems of the womb. Reading between the lines
one could see that repressed sexuality played an important part. As
a result treatment focused on 'discharge', and since masturbation
was taboo and not every woman was eligible for marriage, the
doctors had a part to play. The left-over women were fairly
regularly 'treated' with genital massage. The doctors got little
enjoyment from it, and the medical literature is full of grumbles
about how time-consuming and dreary it was.

Most of the work was delegated to midwives, but it is not
known what attitude that professional group took.

Ultimately it was not the doctors but the general public that
constituted the most interesting target group for manufacturers.
The oldest advert for a home vibrator – the 'Vibration' – dates
from 1899. In these adverts the vibrator took its place alongside
the sewing machine, the kettle and the toaster; housewives still
had ten years to wait for the vacuum cleaner and the iron. The
advert for that first vibrator speaks of the treatment of neuralgia,

headache and wrinkles. Beauty and health were mentioned in the same breath, but the possible sexual uses emerge only in veiled terms.

In *Bilderlexicon Sexualwissenschaft*, an encyclopaedic reference work of 1930, we find that a masturbation machine had been developed in Vienna. Women could operate it for themselves with a foot pedal. Once discovered the machine was confiscated by the police. I was unable to establish in what year this took place, but the apparatus may possibly be found in Dresden in a museum on the history of crime.

The dildo, the godemiché and the masturbation machine all date from long before the invention of the battery. A more recent aid is the *dental dam*. I quote from a feminist monthly: 'A flesh-coloured (white or coloured) rectangular patch, which can be placed between the genitalia and the mouth of the lover. This means that wounds and/or menstrual blood will not be a hazard during sex.'

The last comment points to the fact that the dental dam offers protection against AIDS infection. The item in question was originally designed in America for dentists to mask teeth and so reduce the risk. In practice it turned out to have a different use.

Masturbation machine for women designed in Vienna.

When used the patch created a vacuum, producing a pleasant sexual feeling – and not only in the area of the mouth. According to reports dental dams are also sometimes used by heterosexual couples where the man finds genital kissing repellent. It is said to give an unforgettably intense sensation if one creates a vacuum around the clitoris with what is sometimes called a 'dyke's condom'.

Men on sex aids

Heterosexual men are interested scarcely if at all in dildos and vibrators, and usually dislike them. The Enlightenment poet Willem Bilderdijk (1756–1831) devoted a poem to the subject as early as 1800:

'INSUFFICIENT PLEASURE'

What is it, Sylvia? What lewdness makes you play,
caressing your own body so?
Just how far are you willing to go
to drive your torment away?
In your belly that's bared to our view you place
an imitation male stave,
sheathed in a soft velvet case –
a present some artist gave.
You thrust it up and down and open your thighs wide,
Your nether parts all undulation;
But should they have such a pipe inside?
Does a little milk give natural stimulation?
No! This is mere fake. Choose a lusty lad to ride,
choose me, and I'll provide a spicier sensation!

A story by Yvonne Kroonenberg from her collection *Can I Exchange Him?* also shows men's extreme suspicion about vibrators. The author had lent her old vibrator, which had wound up in the needlework basket, to a woman friend and ordered some new ones for herself. Her own lover had looked on suspiciously as she had unpacked the new collection and her friend's partner had been downright hostile:

'I've got a fight on my hands,' she said. She had come home with the vibrator and shown it to her husband. 'Nice, isn't it?' she had said, but her husband was furious. 'Either that goes, or I go!' he had said.

'A shame,' I said, 'because I've got a whole nest of vibrators, and you can try them all, except for one, which is mine.' I looked at the low table on which my range of equipment was displayed.

Shortly afterwards she sat there with the black vibrator in her hand. At her feet was a plastic bag full of test items. She was going to try out Tarzan and the silver balls. She was taking the harmonica for her sister. I was to keep the butterfly and the small accessories, as I'm not very fond of vibrators for internal use.

'Black men don't have black pricks at all,' said my friend, 'this is completely the wrong colour, it's black minstrel black.'

'I think it's too big,' I said, 'I don't think any woman could cope with that thing.'

'Mmm,' said my friend, 'you'd be surprised.'

'And I don't like the feel of it, all sticky.'

'It feels very realistic,' said my friend, 'sort of halfway between hard and soft. It feels warm if you hold it in your hand for a bit and it really is a bit sticky. Just like the real thing.' A dreamy look came into her eyes.

It was not until years after this story was written that it emerged that the realistic, soft, black silicon rubber Tarzan contained so-called plasticizers, carcinogenic substances which were added to the toys during manufacture, mostly in China. Nowadays there is some monitoring in the industry, but insiders tell me inferior merchandise is still sold.

Another aspect is hygiene. You throw condoms away and you can wash a vibrator, but can't the material develop cracks that bacteria can get into? Eventually many vibrators may literally come alive . . . The reader may have deduced from this that the writer himself doesn't have much use for vibrators. This has nothing to do with the fear of being dumped by my partner. True, some men think that masturbation weakens a woman's desire for sex with her partner, but that is quite simply not so. The subject has been researched by Greenberg and others, and they showed unambiguously that there is no demonstrable relation between the number of times a woman masturbates and the frequency of intercourse with her partner. Most women who masturbate obviously have sufficient energy not to sell their partner short.

It is odd that society should act as if the taboo on vibrators had disappeared once and for all. In the 1960s they were bought as 'massage sticks'. Right at the back of the mail order catalogue, after garden tools, there was a photograph of a lady with a friendly smile holding a white stick against her cheek. Later one had to go to sex shops for them, tacky establishments with a plush velvet curtain over the entrance. Behind the actual shop there was usually a video room with semen stains on the red carpet. Most sex shops had an air of despair and loneliness about them that often put off people who enjoyed sex.

Nowadays in some Western countries there are brightly coloured vibrators, with such names as Petit, Superb and Magnifique, on display in different sizes on the chemist's shelves. Yet many women still walk past with a shrug of the shoulders. The day when women can say to each other: 'I masturbated yesterday and it was fantastic, shall I tell you how?' is still a long way off.

Online shopping

In 2007 there was a controversy about an ad for a vibrator in the Mother's Day brochure of a major online retailer. Many customers had been offended! They felt that chain was suggesting in its promotional material that it is quite normal for children to give their mother a dildo as a present.

The company devoted a full page to its sex range. This included 'silicon vaginal love balls', coloured and perfumed condoms and a 'super-quiet, innovative stimulator'. On the internet forum of a TV programme customers were up in arms: 'For Christ's sake, you don't buy one of those for your mother.' The company said it was absolutely not their intention to suggest this as a gift for children to give. 'With these items we are targeting partners who want to spoil their wife on Mother's Day,' they protested. 'But,' objected the Child Consumer Foundation, 'this is a public brochure, and is definitely looked at by children.'

The brochure was delivered to 5 million households. Mr Delver, director of the foundation, was certain that unsuspecting children would consult the Mother's Day brochure in search of inspiration for a present. 'Unbelievable,' said Delver, 'a serious miscalculation by the company. It's right that people should complain. They should simply phone.' In his view children did want to have anything to do with their mother's sexual activities. 'In our modern society they are already exposed to sex too early and too frequently. We shouldn't treat our children so frivolously.'

Feelings of shame and guilt are interwoven, and many profound statements have been made, especially on the latter aspect. In *Women's Experience of Sex* (1983) Sheila Kitzinger blamed the guilt about solitary sex on the fear of draining 'vitality from our main duties: satisfying men and rearing children. And 'women not only feel guilty about masturbation but now also feel guilty about being guilty.' This sort of nonsense drives one to distraction!

Fear of softening of the bone marrow or the scourge of God has given way, then, to self-generated spectres. According to Sheila Kitzinger many women are afraid that their vagina will become enlarged or deformed by masturbation and dread becoming addicted, thus losing the desire for sex with their partner. There are also women who think the number of orgasms in their lives is limited, like the number of ova, and that the supply can therefore 'run out' as a result of auto-eroticism – notions based on the ancient theory of scarcity.

Women and girls do not masturbate only with dildos or vibrators. Urologists and gynaecologists are sometimes forced to operate to remove all kinds of objects used to heighten sexual sensation. There is nothing new under the sun: as early as the mid-nineteenth century (1862) a German surgeon invented an ingenious instrument for removing hairpins from the female bladder. The English surgeon Lawson Tait observed that bladder stones often occurred as the result of a hairpin, which he strongly suspected had been inserted while masturbating.

In ten different cases I have removed hairpins from the female bladder that were encrusted with phosphate, and not one of the owners was prepared to give any account of the incident.

A colleague of mine lists the many objects that have been used for masturbation in the course of time: crochet hooks, pencils, carrots, cotton spools and wax candles. In the nineteenth century married women apparently preferred fir cones, artificial penises made of crackling, hair cream jars and drinking glasses. The most amusing combination he found was a hair cream jar and a cockchafer!

Back to the vibrator. Clearly, the massage stick has achieved quite a prominent place in society in the last forty years. The vibrator is extolled as a reliable, superior love. In the TV series *Sex and the City* it was the focus of a string of episodes, and one of the quartet of women friends obviously suffered from vibrator addiction. But little is known about vibrators' prevalence or use. Recently Debra Herbenick and co-workers examined the recent prevalence of women's vibrator use during masturbation and partnered sex in the US in the *Journal of Sexual Medicine*. A representative sample of 3,800 women aged between 18 to 60 was invited to participate in an internet-based survey and 54 per cent participated. The prevalence of vibrator use was found to be 52.5 per cent. Vibrator use was positively related to desire, arousal, vaginal lubrication and orgasm with recent vibrator users scoring higher on most sexual function domains, indicating more positive sexual function. Most women (71.5 per cent) reported having never experienced genital arousal associated with vibrator use. So, in the US vibrator use among women is common, associated with health-promoting behaviours and positive sexual function, and rarely associated with side effects. Apart from that there are a large number of women who want nothing to do with them . . .

Relatively little has been written about sex aids for heterosexual men. We know that some of these men use engine oil or compost when masturbating, but in general aids are usually associated with women and homosexual men. The question arises as to what extent that is true. Unfortunately I was unable to obtain specific sales figures. In the case of heterosexual men we are of course less concerned with vibrators than with inflatable dolls, artificial vaginas, suction pumps, French ticklers and cock rings. 'Men need have no more problems with "puller's aim"', proclaims one brochure, 'since the Virgin Vagina takes all the work off your hands', and 'before you know it the Virgin Vagina will be your very own sex buddy and you can indulge the most sensual fantasies. The Virgin Vagina is a perfect fit for every size of penis, and especially with a little lubricant the experience is almost better than the real thing.'

Inflatable dolls are not only used by lonely men. There are also permanent couples who share their love doll, for threesomes or what have you. 'Bring your girlfriend over for an evening's exciting romp with Cleopatra', suggests a manufacturer's publicity.

According to connoisseurs the inflated Cleopatra knows exactly what men and women want. She turns out to be much naughtier than one might think at first sight. The Cleopatra Love Doll, the packaging of which is pyramid-shaped, has three orifices for sexual use – oral, vaginal and anal. Purchasers receive free lubricant, 'because without it you don't stand a chance with her'.

One sex aid used by numerous men is the noose – for auto-erotic asphyxiation! In the United States alone between five hundred and a thousand people per year die of auto-erotic hanging. Interruption of the oxygen supply to the brain intensifies orgasm. At the moment when oxygen deprivation becomes acute a signal is given to release the noose. Unfortunately oxygen deprivation can also at the same time result in someone no longer being able to make the right decisions or move normally. It is all a matter of seconds, and those precious moments are frequently lost when someone is experiencing orgasm. For example, it may prove impossible to loosen the knot tied, resulting in a slow, painful death. One feels for the next of kin, who are forced to see their loved one dangling naked from a noose of his own making.

The Butt Plug Gnome

The 'Butt Plug Gnome', as the 5-metre-high statue costing almost 300,000 euros came to be known popularly in Rotterdam, had already been rejected for various locations, because of the string-bound Christmas tree resembling a sex aid in the figure's hand. Butt plugs are familiar to gay men, and are considered important enough to have their own entry on Wikipedia. 'A butt plug is a sex toy designed to be inserted in the anus and rectum for sexual pleasure. In some ways they are similar to a dildo, but they tend to be shorter, and to have a flared end to prevent the device from being lost inside the rectum.' Men experience a pleasant sensation

'Santa Claus' or 'The Butt
Plug Gnome', photographed
in Museum Park.

from a butt plug because it stimulates the prostate, while in women
it affects the deeper layers of the clitoris, though opinion is divided
on its effect on women.

On Friday 28 November 2008, after years of squabbling, the
huge work 'Santa Claus', aka 'The Butt Plug Gnome' finally found
a permanent home. Scores of children, dressed as gnomes, accompanied the statue from the Boijmans Van Beuningen Museum
where it had been given sanctuary for many years. The business
community largely welcomed the move!

The municipality of Rotterdam had commissioned the bronze
sculpture in 2001 from the American artist Paul McCarthy. The
work is an indictment of consumer society. 'Santa Claus' is the
artist's protest against hysterical consumer behaviour. The statue
was originally designed for the shopping precinct near the city's
concert hall, but there was considerable protest in the town council. It was argued that the public would be offended by the work,
which quickly became known as a sex gnome, while some saw the
object he was holding in one hand as a sex toy.

The art historian Jan Adrichem was a member of the commissioning committee. He expressed his pleasure that Santa Claus
would finally be given a good spot. 'It's about time all the hooha

stopped', he said. 'We thought all along that Rotterdam could take a statue like this, but things turned out differently. It provoked lots of reactions and that's a good thing.'

'They're taking a risk with that central location,' some shopkeepers in the street felt. 'A family from the Bible Belt are going to walk the other way when they see the statue,' said a florist. 'Not all,' retorted a passer-by who had just bought a bunch of flowers, 'people like that don't even know what it represents.'

Actually, criticism of the statue did not abate. An ordinary Rotterdammer of the sort you can find any day of the week in the city centre said, 'It means nothing at all. It's a waste of money and now it's been given a prime location to show off how ugly it is.' Another said, more subtly: 'It makes an impact, no one can deny that.' The owner of a doughnut stall on the square cleverly exploited the statue, by selling gnomes with doughnuts in the shape of a butt plug!

Undoubtedly, butt plug angst must have begun at some point in the early 1990s with Jeff Koons, who had borrowed it from pornography.

Horses

Masturbation, as I indicated in discussing Anna Enquist's poem, is not really a good term, since it does not always involve the hand. For instance, it has been known for centuries that horse-riding can lead to sexual arousal, particularly in girls, sometimes resulting in orgasm through stimulation of the clitoris. The snag about this is that repeated contact of the clitoris with the hard saddle may cause minor haemorrhaging in the erectile tissue. Such haemorrhages leave traces in the form of minute calcium deposits (*microcalcifications*), which disrupts the microarchitecture of the clitoris. This can be demonstrated by ultrasound, as was done by two Italian female researchers from Bologna, not only for horse-women but also for female mountainbikers (*Journal of Sexual*

Medicine, February 2009). The latter group experience the same problems after practising their sport for an extended period: pain in the crotch, frequent need to urinate, pain when urinating and, if they are unlucky, boils. Conclusion: excessive pursuit of sport is no good at all for one's sex life.

Perhaps the fact that many horsewomen can easily reach orgasm is also connected with their well developed pelvic floor muscles. Ever heard of 'core-gasm'? That means coming in the gym instead of in a horse box at the riding school. It is an orgasm that you feel with your whole body. There are women who experience total pleasure while working out. When a woman is exercising she produces endorphins and dopamine, substances which are necessary for orgasm. It happens most frequently with women with very strong pelvic floor muscles, sometimes called the suction muscles. If they train these they can reach a climax more easily, or at least so it is claimed by scientists Graber and Kline-Graber in *The Journal of Clinical Psychiatry* (1979).

Returning to horse-riding: this activity can also prematurely rupture the hymen. I came across the following theory on masturbation and horse-riding by girls on the internet:

> For some years I have been trying to secure a hearing for my theory in the world, but without any success. Time after time I am disbelieved, dismissed and declared to be a salacious nutcase. I let it rest for a while, until I suffered from a severe shortage of interesting topics for my website. So once again I shall try to give the world the benefit of my knowledge of little girls who ride horses. My thesis is as follows: girls love riding. With few exceptions, all girls' mouths water at the thought of a real horse (or even worse, a pony) of their own and they stare dreamily into space while reading their diaries. But why? Quite simply because horses turn them on.
>
> Hey, don't stop reading. I don't mean that that little girls actually want to have sex with horses, not at all. Although, so

my sources tell me, some cases have been recorded. The girls are turned on by horseriding, the jogging up and down. For that matter, so are all women, since you retain a fetish throughout your life.

And think about it logically for a second. The clitoris is after all central to a woman's experience of orgasm and as a man you should stimulate it if you can find time amid all the other things you have to do (beer drinking?). During riding this clitoris is smacked against a hard saddle, or even better against a warm mass of horse flesh of a hundred-plus kilos called a horse, with the force of gravity. So is it odd to maintain that such a thing arouses a woman sexually?

But, as women always do, they will fight against this and deny it. They say that they think horses are beautiful animals, which of course is total nonsense, since a horse is only beautiful when it's on a barbecue, when it also smells better.

That denial is partly due to the fact that while riding little girls cannot put those 'nice feelings' in the 'sexual pleasure' pigeonhole. Only later, when it is too late to link 'equestrian masturbation' to sex, do they actually start to feel about it like that. But it's no big deal that they deny, because it's a wonderful way for them to be run in. Like tenderising meat . . .

It was known as long ago as the nineteenth century that hobby horses could sexually excite girls. Sigmund Freud referred to it in *Three Essays on Sexuality*, and specifically to the sexual pleasure of rocking itself. And what are we to make of children who are far too keen too 'play horsie' on their father or mother's knee. It obviously gives pleasure and as long as it does not trigger any weird fantasies in the parent, it is an innocent activity.

A good orgasm is beyond price

In May 2009 a major daily carried an article headed 'A Good Orgasm is Beyond Price'. Its subject was a medical procedure designed to help women achieve a better climax. 'The hypodermic is inserted in the slightly anaesthetized vagina for eight seconds in order to inject 1.5 cc of collagen. After three hours you can think about sex again, this time with an enlarged G spot. This erogenous zone will now measure about 2 centimetres, and can be bigger if one wishes. In that case you go for a double shot', says Dr David Matlock. He is the founder of the Laser Vaginal Rejuvenation Institute of Los Angeles, and also the inventor and promoter of this growing form of cosmetic surgery known as the G shot.

'It takes fifteen minutes in all; you can have it done in your lunchtime. We have asked women whether it helped and 87 per cent said yes. A "single shot" costs $1,850, a double $2,500 and both last about four months. The procedure is gaining in popularity. Doctors buy the kit and receive their instructions on-line within thirty minutes,' says Matlock.

The article reported that doctors in 39 American states were offering treatment based on the discovery. Not everyone was as enthusiastic about the effect as Matlock. 'Certainly there are colleagues in the Netherlands who enlarge the G spot, one of them on his own testimony scores of times a month,' commented a professor of aesthetic surgery at Groningen University Medical Centre. 'If you're doing something out of the ordinary, that attracts attention. Perhaps some women like it and find it enhances their pleasure. Whether it helps, I've no idea. Perhaps it has a psychological effect.' The surgeon pleaded for caution. 'The use of a one-off filler would certainly be unsafe, since your body is constantly changing. It would be safer to inject natural collagen or hyaluronic acid regularly, in the same way as they are used in the skin as an anti-wrinkle filler. I know of no long-term studies that show a proven effect of G-spot enlargement through injection. For that reason I would not embark on such a procedure.' Caution is important, he thinks. 'Surgery can't solve everything.'

Rik van Lunsen, a sexologist working at the Amsterdam Medical Centre, also knew of the treatment, 'I think it's charlatanism and quack medicine. The G spot isn't an anatomical principle, it's a myth. We know that some women derive pleasure from stimulation of the front wall of the vagina. It contains a large number of nerve ends and sensitivity is greatest there. Other women find it unpleasant or painful. Compare it with the nipple or the ear lobe. Whether or not it is a hot spot varies from person to person.'

David Matlock did think that all women have such a spot. 'It's a matter of experience and knowledge. I get no criticism from women. I do from men, though. For men millions have been spent on medical advances like Viagra. Research on women is lagging behind. I do this for healthy women who choose for themselves. It's cosmetic surgery. If you don't want it, you don't have to have it.'

Another invention turned out to originate from Vienna. Muscle workouts between the legs helps one reach orgasm more often, according to Austrian sexologist Dr Karl Stifter. 'German research showed that 44% of women would like more frequent orgasms. And I'd like to make them happier.' He explains: 'The vagina is like a hollow muscle, which when excited swells like a balloon. This makes it difficult for the penis to reach the erogenous zones: the 'lost-penis syndrome'. With proper training the vagina folds around the penis like an envelope, and so one can reach the G spot, for instance, more easily.'

Strengthening the pelvic floor muscles, Stifter believes, is woman's way to improved orgasms. 'We've known for a long time, but the case of some exercises it's not clear if you're training the correct movement, or else they take 2.5 hours a day.'

Things must be simplified, in Stifter's view. His solution, which is now available worldwide, came from sports science a few years ago. 'I devised a muscle-toning programme like you have at the gym.'

A 'vaginal work-out' twice a day in which the pelvic floor is contracted for a few minutes with the help of a training aid, the COME, Clinical Orgasm Muscle Exerciser. 'You can stop the moment you feel your muscles getting tired, as you do at the gym,' said the inventor in the interview.

Again sexologist Rik van Lunsen was unimpressed. 'The striking thing is that these kinds of technical solution, like the G shot, for ordinary healthy women, are always invented by men.' 'Physiotherapy with a specialist pelvic physio sometimes makes sense,' he admitted, 'if a woman has an incredibly slack or else an over-taut pelvic floor. And certainly those muscles contract during orgasm and play an important part. But what you need is a supple and dynamic pelvic floor. If you overtrain to achieve flexing of the pelvic floor muscles and pay too little attention to relaxing them, you cause all kind of sexual problems, like pain and the inability to become sufficiently moist. But can we now say that there are technical solutions? Seldom if ever. This kind of stuff is genital plumbing. It's quite simply easier for patients and for doctors to look at a quick so-called solution than to talk at the personal level about intimacy, feelings, fantasies and how to get to know your own body better.'

In the Netherlands 85 per cent of eighteen-year-old girls can achieve orgasm through masturbation. Van Lunsen: 'If you want to be sure of an orgasm, you have to do it by yourself. If you want to do it with a partner, then you must say what you like, and be able to let yourself go. In sex with a partner there is a moment to go your own way, to release yourself into your own feelings.' Good advice!

Anal stimulation

Men masturbate in the oddest places. A Swedish newspaper reported in 2008: 'A 36-year-old man was up in court on a charge of having masturbated on women's bike saddles. The police found semen on a saddle and a little later he was caught red-handed by a woman.' The police had been on his trail since they had been called out because of a wrecked bike, and for the first time saw a strange stain on the saddle. Shortly afterwards a woman reported that a man was masturbating on her bike and he was picked up. The man confessed and stated that it had a calming effect on him to masturbate on the saddles of women's bikes . . . Well, well.

Not only gay men but straight men too, while jerking off with one hand, enjoy sticking the index finger of their other hand in their anus. On the internet there are many forums where all kinds of methods are discussed. 'Tomtom' wrote:

> Hi, I like playing with my arse. Normally I'm not so open about it, but in the anonymity of this forum I hope to pick up some tips and experiences.
>
> I usually start massaging my anus with my fingers and some oil or lubricant. Then I carefully insert a finger and let it warm up a bit. It's not always very clean inside, which is why the bathroom is a favourite spot for this game. I rinse myself clean with the showerhead. But if I'm feeling kinky I scrape out the faeces with a finger, with or without latex gloves. When everything is clean all that comes out are often soft, thick juices that also act as a lubricant. I stick another finger in and if it still goes smoothly with two fingers it's time to get out the sex aids. I've tried everything, from vegetables and fruit to rubber toys, but I like the toys best. My favourite is a number of plastic beads on a thick plastic cord. It's not that thick but it gives a wonderful feeling.

Let's be clear about it: men masturbate with a wide variety of different objects, especially homosexual men. An object is inserted in the anus and may accidentally shoot upwards and end up in the rectum, and then the fat is in the fire! In 2008 researchers

Koornstra and Weersma published an article on their experiences and gave an overview of others' findings. They were concerned not only with the objects themselves but with ways of extracting them. This was done, for example, manually, naturally after stretching the anus, with various kinds of forceps, an electro-magnet, a kind of corkscrew, a vacuum pump normally used in labour, a plaster of Paris filling – in the case of a vase – and catheters. The catheter was inserted to the side of the foreign body, after which a balloon was inflated to enable the object to be hooked and removed.

Objects removed included the previously mentioned vase, a ballpoint pen, a balloon filled with water, a chicken bone, a tooth-pick, a glass bottle, a working vibrator, a glass rod, a blow pipe, a pencil, an iron bar, a bottleneck, various kinds of spray cans, aftershave, an apple, a light bulb, a thermometer, a piece of wood, an oven glove, a zinc drainpipe, a carrot, a rubber ball, a pocket torch and, inevitably, a dildo.

Fortunately an operation is rarely necessary, though anaesthetic is often required to help the abdominal muscles relax completely. The doctor can then press on the abdomen and at the same time take hold of the object with his hand via the anus. As a precaution the intestine is then inspected for possible damage. It is best if such patients spend as little time as possible in hospital, since they are regarded with disapproval by many members of staff.

Artificial ejaculation

Vibrators are also the subject of some debate in medical circles. This centres on treatment of what is called *anejaculation*, the inability to achieve ejaculation. This may have psychological causes, but the use of certain medication, operations, spinal cord lesions and other neurological conditions may also be at the root of the problem. The problem represents a serious dysfunction. If ejaculation cannot be induced through medication, vibro-ejaculation is indicated. This is done with a very powerful vibrator (at a preferred setting of 80–120 Herz, amplitude between 1.5 and 2.2 millimetres, which is especially effective with men in whom the ejaculation centre in the spinal cord and the sacral reflex arc have remained intact. The vibrator is placed on the frenulum linking the head of the penis and the foreskin. If the device is properly set up, 'normal' men reach ejaculation in no time at all; with patients the success rate is around 70 per cent.

Electro-ejaculation is an important therapeutic option for men with an ejaculation dysfunction with whom medication therapy and the use of a 'medical' vibrator have failed. These are usually patients with a spinal cord lesion, multiple sclerosis, diabetes, spina bifida (patients born with an 'open' spine) or psychogenic anejaculation.

The first publication of the clinical use of electro-ejaculation dates from 1948. Before that time the technique was used by veterinary surgeons in zoos to obtain semen from, for example, a tiger, for subsequent use on the other side of the world to inseminate a female. This was a way of avoiding inbreeding and worldwide breeding programmes were set up.

Using electro-ejaculation sperm can be obtained from 90 per cent of patients. The quality of that sperm is variable, and the mobility of the spermatozoa is generally poor, meaning that the percentage of pregnancies is low. Possible causes include 'stale', that is, old sperm, obstructions in the epididymis, in the case of spinal cord lesion patients too high a temperature in the scrotum, and perhaps the effect of the electro-ejaculation itself. Generally several sessions are needed to gather sufficient material. If electro-ejaculation is not successful, sperm cells can be direct extracted from the epididymis using suction. This can be carried out under local anaesthetic, but many patients prefer general anaesthetic, so that the procedure is gradually coming to be called an operation.

The volume, smell and taste of sperm

Masturbation is the ideal opportunity to have a good look at the ejaculate, and many young men and women seize that opportunity. They see all kinds of things, but want explanations.

Well then, what are the facts? The quantity of sperm ejaculated by a man varies from 2 to 4 millilitres, that is, after sexual abstinence of between 24 and 36 hours. A modest amount compared with what a pig (boar) produces: approximately half a litre each time, as I was once told by a veterinary surgeon. Don't let us get into details about zebras. After they have mated and the stallion withdraws his penis from the vagina, it looks as if the mare has become incontinent: the sperm comes pouring out! According to one American urologist, the world record for human beings is half a teacupful. In the making of porn films, by the way, it is customary for the actor who has to ejaculate to abstain from sex for a few days, to ensure that the amount of ejaculate in the film is as large as possible.

If one asks a man how many millilitres he ejaculates each time, he will usually overestimate. The same applies to the members of a well-known 1970s pop group; they called themselves 10 CC, after the estimated amount.

Immediately after ejaculation the sperm coagulates. It looks rather clotted, like the white of an egg that has been heated for a second. After a quarter of an hour this jelly liquefies again.

The greater part of the volume of sperm is produced by the two seminal vesicles and the prostate gland. The vesicles are situated on either side of the back of the prostate. They issue directly into the seminal ducts, just before they enter the prostate. They provide between 70 per cent and 80 per cent of the seminal fluid. This is a clear fluid and contains a large amount of fructose, which gives it a rather syrupy texture.

The seminal ducts run diagonally through the prostate and issue into the urethra. Between 20 per cent and 30 per cent of the sperm volume is produced in the prostate. The prostate liquid gives the sperm its milky-white colour, sometimes tending to yellow.

While the seed is being expelled the neck of the bladder is closed, to prevent the semen being forced into the bladder. In fact after a prostate operation, the neck of the bladder simply cannot close. Such a procedure does irreparable damage to the closure mechanism, and the sperm is simply expelled with the urine.

As one gets older there is sometimes a marked loss of sensation on ejaculation. As with other physiological processes, one runs out of steam! There is a joke about it: An old man consults his GP because he has noticed some white secretions from his penis in the mornings. 'How old are you?' asks the doctor.

'Seventy-two,' replies the man, adding that he hasn't had any sexual relations for a month.

'But you did have a month ago?' asks the doctor.

'Yes.'

'Well, that's it – you're coming!'

The smell of sperm is often compared by women to plant or flower odours. Herb Robert (*Geranium robertianum*), St John's wort (*Hypericum perforatum*), the flowers of the European barberry (*Berberis vulgaris*) and chestnut all smell of sperm. The same goes for the crushed flowers of the henna plant (*Lawsonia inermis*). Moroccan women love rubbing this into their palms, while Western European women use it to dye their hair.

Billygoats drench their own beards with sperm and urine, as a sign of sexual potency to females. From time immemorial billygoats have been regarded as the prototype of animal lust. Moreover, the ancient Greeks dreamt up all kinds of hybrid beings consisting of man and billygoat, such as the demigod satyr and the forest god Pan. The physical attributes of these sensual figures (horns, cloven hooves, beard) were adopted by Christianity to depict the devil. However, billygoats have surprisingly feminine traits: if their nipples are massaged at length a milk-yielding udder appears in front of the scrotum!

The American jazz musician Charles Mingus compared sperm to cream: 'She gulps and slurps the cream out of me while I melt and she sucks hard at my tree.' John Hunter, a nineteenth-century English surgeon, observed in an essay that 'if one keeps sperm in one's mouth it produces a warmth similar to spices'. The celebrated sexologist Havelock Ellis wrote in one of his many books that many peoples, especially the Australian Aborigines, make drinks from sperm, which are then given to sick or dying members of the tribe. He also mentions the Manichaeans and the Albigensian sect, who sprinkled the bread used for Holy Communion with human sperm. In the seventeenth century sperm was regarded as a powerful defence against magic and a precious aphrodisiac. However, the Church refused to sanction it and in his book Ellis mentions prison sentences of seven years for offenders.

Internet names for sperm include: jizz, spunk, cum, man milk, love juice, home-made yoghurt, mayo, boner brew, salt malt, cream, baby juice, load, skeet, cocknog, nut-nectar, spooge and liquid sin.

I have it on good authority that it is not unusual for young women today in a get-together in the pub to admit whether or not they 'swallow'. They're not talking about E, amphetamines or such-like, but about whether or not they swallow sperm. There is some similarity between sucking and fellatio, between mother's milk and sperm: just as an infant can taste whether its mother has eaten garlic, a woman who 'swallows' can taste whether her man has eaten garlic the day before. Sperm is both stronger in flavour and more bitter if a man smokes and drinks a lot of coffee while the sperm of vegetarians reputedly tastes better than that of carni-vores. Kiwi fruit particularly are supposed to improve the flavour.

While we are talking about ejaculation and secretion, this is the place to mention in passing the glands about which the Eng-lish physician William Cowper was the first to publish in 1702, situated a little downstream from the prostate and also issuing into the urethra, which in a state of arousal produce the so-called pre-seminal fluid. In women these glands are named after the Danish researcher Bartholin.

From the above one can infer that the smell of sperm is immediately recognizable to many of us. A well-known story on the subject related to the imprisonment of the Irish writer and poet Oscar Wilde in Wandsworth Prison from 1894 to 1900, and the incident took place in 1895. Some years earlier the writer had met Lord Alfred Douglas, the son of the Marquess of Queensberry. The two men fell madly in love, despite the fact that Wilde was married. Douglas's father wanted them to end the relationship, and in 1895 he accused Wilde of sodomy (homosexuality), to which Wilde responded by beginning proceedings against the Marquess for defamation. The court, however, found in favour of Queensberry. Although Wilde had the chance to flee to France, he chose not to do so, and was subsequently arrested and imprisoned.

According to the story the deputy prison chaplain, called W. D. Morrison, literally and figuratively smelled a rat. He wrote that the stench in Wilde's cell was unbearable and that the guards had to clean it every day with carbolic acid. 'I fear that on the basis of what I have seen and heard that perverse sexual practices are being pursued in the cell', he wrote, 'and that in view of the smell masturbation must be involved.' The authorities, however, denied emphatically that Wilde had turned into a chronic masturbator in their charge, and the poor chaplain was transferred!

The fact that he had recognized the smell is actually no surprise. The odour of sperm is familiar to every man: it is the smell of non-procreative sex, the smell of masturbation or homosexual encounters. The recognition implies an admission that at some time or other one has engaged in such a form of sex.

Back to Wilde. His health suffered as a result of his imprisonment and he spent the last years of his life in poverty in France, where he died of meningitis at the age of 46. He is buried in the cemetery of Père-Lachaise in Paris. The angel on his famous headstone by the British sculptor Jacob Epstein had its testicles chiselled off by vandals.

Bill Clinton

Not so long ago psychologists Bockting and Coleman attempted to make a contribution towards breaking the taboo on masturbation. The book *Masturbation as a Means of Achieving Sexual Health* (2002) was the product of a conference on the subject organized by the Midcontinent Region of the Society for the Scientific Study of Sexuality. Do you masturbate? If so, how often and to what extent do you feel guilty about it? The participants met mainly to devise less traditional questions and to set up a kind of research agenda. In his introduction Bockting wrote that it had been quite a job afterwards to actually get people to send manuscripts of the lectures given!

Bockting is Dutch by birth and obtained his doctorate from the Free University of Amsterdam. He writes about his background in the introduction. 'However, perhaps in part because of my background as a native from the Netherlands, a country known for sexual tolerance and freedom, I was astounded to discover that discussing masturbation as part of promoting safer sex was deemed inappropriate.'

In the first chapter his co-editor Coleman spells out, for example, that modern sexologists of course try through education, care and information to eliminate negative attitudes to masturbation and on the contrary to emphasize the pleasurable and liberating aspects. But in his view there has been insufficient research into the ways in which people masturbate and it remains unclear whether it does any good. Based on old American research (from 1948 and 1949) Coleman argues that with masturbation there are differences based on race, socio-economic class, level of education and religious background and that more research should be devoted to it. Those Dutch people who have remained in the Netherlands have known for ages, thanks to opinion polls, that there are differences in their small country on that score.

What is the relation between fantasy and masturbation? What are the effects of sex education? Coleman raises many questions. He reminds the reader that Joycelyn Elders, Surgeon General in the US Health Department, was asked by Bill Clinton in person to resign after she had said in 1994 on World AIDS Day that masturbation was an alternative to sexual intercourse, if one wished to avoid AIDS infection. 'Masturbation is a part of human sexuality, and it's a part of something that perhaps should be taught. But we have not even taught our children the basics. And I feel that we have tried ignorance for a long time and it is time we tried education.' This cost Joycelyn Elders her job. She planned to return to the Medical School of the University of Arkansas as Professor of Paediatrics, but conservative members of Congress attempted to prevent her. When the budget of this university was approved by the budget committee of the House of Congress, Congressman Ted Mullenix from Pearcy, Arkansas, said that he did not consider it in the state's interest to allow Dr Elders to return to Arkansas Medical School in order to teach 'those policies'. Mullenix was alluding to Elders' pleas to begin sex education from the earliest grades and to distribute free condoms in schools. Her statements on abortion were very controversial from the start. In 1992 she said that opponents of abortion 'should finally get over their love affair with the foetus' and a year later 'Look at the kind of people who are active in the "Pro-Choice" movement: the celibate, male-dominated Church.' Dr Elders also believes that Medicaid, the US health programme for low-income citizens, should pay for abortion for poor women.

Responding to Congressman Mullenix's statement Elders pointed out that her 'school classes' in Arkansas comprised third and fourth-year medical students, who could surely be considered reasonably worldly people.

Commenting on the affair the prestigious medical journal *The Lancet* wrote that Dr Elders would go down in history as an excellent paediatrician and a very courageous surgeon general, who was dismissed for speaking the truth. The journal considered it high time that masturbation was discussed openly as a normal component of human sexual behaviour. By way of illustration it quoted the ridiculously circuitous way in which masturbation was defined in a British survey of sexual behaviour, the 'National Survey of British Sexual Attitudes and Lifestyles': 'Genital contact with a man (woman), not involving sexual intercourse, for example stimulation of the genitalia with the hand, but not leading to vaginal, oral or anal intercourse.' This formulation was deemed necessary, since a more direct question about masturbation would have been found tasteless and embarrassing by respondents.

The second chapter of *Masturbation as a Way of Achieving Sexual Health* – on the history of thinking about masturbation – is by Vern Bullough, and is extensive and readable. However, the thinking of Freud and the early German sexologists receives little attention. The following chapters are as dry as dust. Sociologists from Hamburg discuss the changes in students' masturbatory behaviour in the period 1966–96 and sociologists from Finland do more or less the same for the inhabitants of Sweden, Finland, Estonia and St Petersburg. This is followed by an endless series of tables with conclusions that in my opinion ought not to have been drawn from what preceded them. American researchers report on research on the relation between masturbatory behaviour and the risk of HIV infection in African-American women. Contrary to the researchers' expectations women who masturbated frequently turned out to have several sexual partners and displayed riskier behaviour. Similar results were found among female students: the earlier they had started masturbating the greater the risk of HIV infection.

The last chapter is devoted to the relation between masturbation and sexual desires, fantasies and activities. It offers a research model for investigating whether masturbation can be used in the treatment of 'hypoactive sexual desire disorder'.

Bockting and Coleman's book does not help to break the taboo on masturbation and is not written in language accessible to the layman. It contains a great deal of jargon. The glossy cover features quite inappropriately, besides the misleading title – I expected an optimistic American instruction manual – such words as 'intimacy', 'orgasm', 'pleasure', 'power', 'autonomy' and 'exploration'. These are empty words, and in fact the book is merely a set of scientific papers under one cover. The papers are fine for setting up a research agenda, but not as a guide to becoming sexually healthy.

5

Animals

Masturbation occurs not only in humans but also in many other mammals, such as dogs, apes (bonobos), kangaroos and elephants – the list is endless. Look at YouTube under 'kangaroo masturbation'.

Most pet owners know that masturbation occurs among bitches and female cats when on heat, who rub their vulvas against all sorts of objects. The males ride on the knees of unsuspecting ladies in miniskirts, while female ferrets use smooth stones. However, my favourite by far are female porcupines in captivity, which sometimes grab a stick with their front legs, which they mount like a broomstick, and then walk around the cage dragging the stick along the ground, so that the jolting and vibrating provide a pleasant stimulus.

In many primates too both sexes masturbate with some regularity, for example the red-capped mangabey, a smoky-coloured ape from West Africa with a long tail and an extravagant amount of hair on its cheeks. Both male and female orangutans excite themselves with sex toys that they fashion from branches and leaves. A female chimpanzee that grew up in a human household masturbated while looking at exciting photos of naked human males. Male red deer do it by rubbing the tips of their antlers along the ground; from start to finish the process takes no more than fifteen seconds. The question is whether there are other males who do it for the same reason as the young marine iguanas discussed by Dr Tatiana.

Female Japanese macaque masturbating.

Dr Tatiana

In her unsurpassed book *Dr Tatiana's Sex Advice to All Creation: The Definitive Guide to the Evolutionary Biology of Sex*, Olivia Judson sketches the masturbatory behaviour of marine iguanas in a question-and-answer game:

> Dear Dr Tatiana,
> I'm a marine iguana, and I'm appalled by the behaviour of the young iguanas of today. I keep encountering groups of youths masturbating at me. It's revolting. I'm sure they didn't dare act this way in Darwin's time. How can I make them stop?
> Disgusted in the Galápagos

To which Tatiana replies:

> I get a lot of letters from young male iguanas, frustrated because the girls ignore them. But this is the first time I've heard complaints from the other side. Look at it from the guy's point of view. Here he is, a tasteful shade of red, his spiky crest a full twenty centimetres from his crown to his tail – he's ready to go, desperate to use one or the other of his penises (yes, like many reptiles, he has two, a left and a right penis). But being

young and therefore small, he doesn't have much of a chance. It isn't just that you ladies prefer to mate with older, bigger males. It's that even if he manages to mount a female, the odds are he'll be shoved aside by a bigger fellow before he climaxes. That's why young males masturbate when they see a girl go by. Wanking reduces the time they need to ejaculate during sex – and thus reduces the risk of being interrupted before their climax. So I'm afraid the behaviour may be here to stay. Young wankers probably sire more children than those who abstain.

So the famous Italian writer Alberto Moravia (1907–1990) was therefore wrong when he maintained that auto-eroticism is the only sexual act that has anything to do with culture, since it springs from the imagination. Equally, Mark Twain (1835–1910) underestimated the sexual playfulness of animals when he wrote that the ape is the only creature apart from man that puts this knowledge into practice and hence is our brother. Every dog-owner could have corrected him on that score. Michael Miersch writes at length about 'masturbation in the animal kingdom' in his book *The Love of Animals*. For a long time biologists were tight-lipped about what they observed in forests and savannahs. Sex, in the commonly held view, was only natural if it served reproductive purposes. For a long period not a word was said about masturbation in books on sex in the animal kingdom.

The French writer Rémy de Gourmont (1858–1915) in his work *The Physics of Love*, published in 1918, devoted only a few sentences to bitches that 'dragged their vulva along the ground' and to 'deer that rub their penises against tree trunks'. Not until 1951 was the taboo broken, when anthropologists Ford and Beach gave graphic depictions of auto-eroticism in the animal kingdom in *Patterns of Sexual Behaviour*.

The zoo director

In 1968 the director of Hanover Zoo published a collection of observations on masturbation. He began with the sentence: 'In a zoo, besides normal heterosexual sexual relationships, one can observe homosexual and sometimes other kinds of abnormal sexual behaviour, mostly masturbation.' Many of the animals described by the director met with an unpleasant end. A female ape suffered a sharp loss of weight and pined away, a half-grown kudu had an accident, a tapir died of tuberculosis, a masturbating ant bear died of exhaustion and the testicles of a sinful elephant degenerated. In the case of a horny and emaciated hippopotamus the director wondered whether there might be a connection between the animal's 'manifold sexual activity' and its weak constitution.

Modern scientists agree: virtually all the higher animals – including parakeets and pigeons – are occasionally involved with their own genitalia and the methods used by the animals vary widely. Grzimek's encyclopaedia of animals mentions wild ibexes, which put the tip of their own penis in their mouths – something that only one in a thousand men can manage! Female hyenas are capable of the same feat with their own, very long clitoris. A male rhinoceros was once observed striking his penis against his abdomen until it ejaculated. Male elephants of course suck on their penises with their trunks and females nibble the nipples located between their front legs and at the same time strike their vulva with their tails. It is said that the dolphins used by the American navy for storing torpedoes rub their genitals against these weapons.

According to Michael Miersch there are indications that primates also fantasize when masturbating. In laboratory experiments an ape was taught to tread on a bar whenever he saw a video film. In its sleep the animal pressed the bar in the same way, while his eyes moved violently beneath his closed eyelids, indicating that the ape was seeing a film in his sleep. The researchers concluded that he was dreaming: after all it is only a short step from dream to sexual fantasy.

Most zoological observations of masturbation derive from mammals and birds, and many of them were made in zoos and laboratories. This does not mean that it is a captivity neurosis; biologists rightly assume that all the behaviours recorded in captivity are also found in the wild. It is, though, quite possible that masturbation is more frequently practised by animals living in a zoo, since no time is wasted chasing about and hunting!

If one is to believe the data, females, just as with humans, do it less often than males. At the same time one should realize that even a scientifically trained observer will record dramatic events quicker and better than unobtrusive behaviour. Few observers will overlook an erect penis and an ejaculation is hard to miss. A female animal can achieve sexual satisfaction without a sound by sliding gently over the ground or rubbing her bottom against a tree trunk, in fact just like a human female. This kind of masturbatory behaviour can simply escape notice.

It is difficult to imagine how masturbation might serve reproduction, and yet this is the case. When a male masturbates, the sperm is fresher the next time he mates. Younger sperm cells are more successful if the spermatozoa of various partners have to compete in a female's body. In the view of biologists Baker and Bellis the masturbator is giving his sperm cells the edge from the outset in the swimming race towards the ovum. It is also argued that masturbation gives female animals a greater chance of reproduction; the muscles around the vagina remain supple and the fluid in the vagina is replenished. Baker and Bellis discovered that women who have intercourse with two partners every few days can influence through masturbation whose sperm will fertilize them. If, for instance, the woman is carrying sperm from Monday inside her, masturbates on Wednesday and has a new lover on Friday, Wednesday's masturbation ensures that Monday's seed is activated and Friday's bedfellow has little or no chance of winning the sperm race.

But apart from socio-biological theory and Darwin's thinking on the struggle for existence, animals can, just like humans, simply derive pleasure from masturbating. The previously quoted zoo director reported the case of a female grey langur (a type of ape) which masturbated with its hand countless times every day, and when reaching a climax 'exhibited almost epileptic, convulsive trembling all over its body'. The director concludes the description of the masturbation-crazed animal with a comparison that must strike a chord with every happy masturbator: 'Neither the prosimians nor other species of apes experience an orgasm of such intensity in normal intercourse.'

The most extensive scientific surveys of masturbation in humans and apes are to be found in the book *Primate Sexuality* by Alan F. Dixson, who devotes seven pages to the subject. It turns out that ape species in the New World do it less frequently than those in the Old World: no logical explanation has been found.

6

Doctors and Other Scientists

If most of us today regard masturbation as an agreeable, enjoyable variant on other forms of physical love, it was assumed well into the nineteenth century that the practice could lead to the most horrific diseases.

Tissot

One of the first doctors to sow panic in this matter was the Swiss Samuel-Auguste Tissot (1728–1797). Probably he was inspired by a book published in 1712 by the English surgeon John Marten, of which more below. Tissot regarded masturbation as a crime, even worse than suicide. Haemorrhoids, constipation, epilepsy, tuberculosis, paralysis and deformed children, were all consequences of this crime. One of his treatment methods was the severing of nerves in the head of the penis.

He adapted an academic thesis on the subject (*Traité de l'Onanisme: Dissertation sur les maladies produites par la masturbation*), which appeared in Latin in 1758 and in French in 1760. The last edition appeared in 1905. Unusually for a thesis it became a huge bestseller. Unsurprisingly, the book is full of amusing exaggerations and admonitions. In the preface Tissot wrote that he preferred not to receive letters or requests for treatment, as he would rather spend his precious time on people who had become ill for an 'honourable' reason. He also described how an onanist's brain could dry out to such an incredible extent that it could be heard rattling in the skull! His theory was as follows: orgasms achieved through masturbation were produced via the imagination, in other words, the brain overheated. If just a quarter of the afflictions and diseases that Tissot assembled with his pathological, sadistic fantasy were real, mankind would long since have died out.

As is clear from other writings of his, Tissot was mainly afraid that the European population would decline too sharply in numbers, not only through emigration to the colonies, but especially through changing lifestyles. For him there was an incontrovertible relationship between the class to which one belonged and one's state of health. Healthiest of all were the peasants, followed by the tradesmen, the bourgeoisie, and finally the 'gens du monde': indolent people with no vocation and too much time on their hands. According to Tissot, boredom drove them to the weirdest behaviour. In his view they were mainly educated people who were concerned solely with the workings of their own minds.

Tissot stressed the preciousness of sperm and described it as an extremely important liquid. He called it the 'essential oil' of all bodily fluids or, to be more exact, 'the *spiritus rector*, which when spilled weakens the others, and in a certain sense leaves them in an evaporated state'. Elsewhere he maintained that sperm was concentrated from blood, so that 'the loss of one ounce of sperm was more debilitating than the loss of forty ounces of blood'. Hence ejaculation caused great damage.

The question that immediately arises, and which Tissot himself in fact posed, is: 'So shouldn't you simply argue that the dangers of masturbation coincide with those of excessive sexual intercourse?' Tissot's answer was that in coitus there was an exchange between two bodies, including 'breath' and 'sweat', both equally essential. The loss of strength was after all less great here than with solitary masturbation, in which in his view all bodily fluids were lost.

The other reasons mentioned by Tissot are, however, at least as interesting, since they relate to the non-physical effects of masturbation, namely emotions such as joy and remorse.

The question is whether these somatic arguments were so important for Tissot himself. It is striking that he refused to express an opinion on crucial points in the medical debates being conducted at the time. This applies, for example, to the question of what sperm actually was: at a time when ovists and animalculists or spermists were in violent disagreement, he contented himself with referring to Hippocrates, Aristotle, Plato and Epicurus, maintaining that the exact nature of sperm was unknown.

In fact, Tissot had become a renowned doctor by ignoring the advice of colleagues and successfully introducing inoculation, the predecessor of vaccination, to combat a deadly epidemic. In addition he was the author of a six-volume work on mental diseases, in which the section on epilepsy was highly regarded by colleagues. So he seems to have been well informed about the advent of neurological science. He was known to the public at large for his booklets on healthy living. So he was not someone who had made a name for himself through his campaign against masturbation, but a famous doctor who happened to write a booklet on masturbation.

There was a trickle of criticism of his writings from medical colleagues, for example from the French surgeon Claude-François Lallemand, but most doctors went along with Tissot's distorted ideas on masturbation. In 1836 Lallemand branded Tissot's book as 'a wretched compilation, lacking critical judgement, full of erroneous and vague theories, deficient observations and often, especially from a therapeutic point of view, lacking discrimination or meaning, and marred by unforgivable errors'. Another major critic was Scottish surgeon John Hunter, who wondered why, if masturbation was so bad for one, so few young people were ill.

Eighteenth-century medicine was a bundle of contradictions. This was the heyday of quackery, and enlightened thinkers were able to force through their attempts at reform only a little at a time in the fossilized medical faculties. The medical establishment doggedly defended its ancient privileges, and had obviously long since forgotten the innovative approach of scientists like Vesalius. In the eighteenth century doctors were far from having an established social position, as Molière's comedies amply demonstrate. Towards the end of the century, however, the French Revolution caused all medical diplomas to be declared null and void, and all medical faculties were closed to be replaced by the new 'Écoles de Médecine'. It was only in the course of the nineteenth century that a single coherent whole, which embraced both theory and practice, emerged. When Tissot was writing, that time was still a long way off. Therefore one cannot conclude from his work that there was great interest in masturbation in medicine *as a whole*. True, Tissot was influential in certain quarters, but not in what would later be recognized as the authentic medical tradition.

At any rate Tissot's ostensibly scientific approach did have a considerable influence on the development of the anti-masturbation movement. Not only doctors, but many clergy and pedagogues accepted his ideas. The masturbation fallacy was certainly grist to the mill of the Catholic Church – the moral theologians could not believe their luck!

Marie Antoinette

The fact that the medical masturbation fallacy of the Enlightenment period was not shared by everyone at the time is clear from the actions of a leading player in the French Revolution, the Count de Mirabeau (1749–1791). He tried to persuade Louis XVI (1754–1793) and his wife Marie Antoinette (1755–1793) of the necessity of reaching a compromise with the supporters of the Revolution, as a damage-limitation exercise. However, partly because of his adventurous past the king and queen had insufficient confidence in him. They did not understand that the intelligent and eloquent Mirabeau was their best hope, and so their fate was sealed.

Mirabeau did not believe the horror stories being disseminated about onanism. He believed Galen's assertions about the toxicological effects of pent-up sperm and hence considered masturbation a sensible act. Queen Marie Antoinette was to experience personally the popular misconception about masturbation in the most disgusting way. Before she was guillotined, her judges sought to justify the execution. The trial records (see André Castelot, *Marie Antoinette*, 1962) record an infamous deception. In the official indictment she is charged – at Robespierre's insistence – not only with high treason but with the following:

> The widow Capet (i.e. Marie Antoinette), immoral in every respect, is so perverse and so acquainted with all vices that she does not even eschew to forget her motherhood and the boundaries imposed by it, and to indulge with Louis-Charles Capet, her son – according to the latter's testimony – in filthy acts, whose image and name make one shiver with dismay.

According to the historian Castelot the prosecution summoned her eight-year-old son, Louis XVII (1785–1795). He had been given into the care of a certain Simon, who was to be responsible for his further upbringing. The poor boy testified that he had been surprised in bed several times by Simon and his wife 'doing indecent things that harm the health'.

It was alleged that his mother had taught him these indecent acts. The witness Hébert made the following statement at the trial:

> The young Capet, whose health was deteriorating day by day, was caught by Simon committing indecent acts of self-pollution that damaged his health. When Simon asked him who had taught him such criminal behaviour, he replied that it was his mother and his aunt. These women regularly had him sleep between them, as emerged from the testimony of the young Capet to the mayor of Paris and the prosecutor of

the Commune. It is likely that this illicit pleasure was taught to the boy not for reasons of sexual pleasure, but rather in the political hope that the child in that way would be physically weakened. For it was still assumed that he would later ascend the throne and it was obviously hoped to exert an influence on him. As a result of these exertions and efforts that he had been taught, the child had suffered a hernia and consequently had to wear a truss. Since the child has been separated from his mother, he is regaining his strength.

This is Hébert's testimony. When asked the meaning of this witness statement, Marie Antoinette replied that she had no idea what the witness was talking about. Natural delicacy forbade her to respond to such an accusation. Many of those present agreed with her.

Ailments caused by onanism

The followers of Tissot were to make the list of ailments caused by masturbation even longer. These included restlessness, particularly at night, emaciation, gloomy expression, absent and quiet, eyes melancholy, features dull, voice hoarse, lazy and listless, diffident around parents, knees trembling, longing for solitude, silent for no reason, shyness and calf cramps. Various kinds of eye disease, pain above the eye sockets, pain at the back of the head, strange sensations above the head, various types of neuralgia, tenderness of the skin above the lower portion of the spine, asthma, heart murmur, blisters on wounds, poor healing of wounds, acne, dilated pupils, strabismus, bags under the eyes, pale and discoloured skin, redness of the nose, convulsive cough, incontinence, warts on the hands, strange-smelling skin and deafness: all of these, according to the doctors, were the result of masturbation.

The interpretation of spinal disorders as a result of masturbation derived from the ideas of Leonardo da Vinci. The most brilliant brain in world history was very interested in the sexual organs, but in his anatomical studies committed no less than two errors. The first was omitting to draw the clitoris. As was seen in a previous chapter, he represented the female genitalia as a great gaping hole. That is all very well, but in the penis he drew two channels, one for urinating and one for ejaculating, fully in line with the views of the Catholic Church. And the latter channel was directly connected to the spinal cord, since in Leonardo's view this was where the 'white substance', or semen was produced. In women he drew direct connections between the breasts and the spinal cord, since mother's milk was also a 'white substance'.

To return to the 'problems' of masturbation: objective phenomena in masturbators were identified by urologists through endoscopy, inspection of the bladder and urethra. In advanced cases the natural, bright red colour of the seminal colliculus changed to scarlet. The tip of the colliculus went white and bled at the merest touch. If strands of mucus could also be detected in the urine, the diagnosis was very definite: onanism.

Causes of onanism

In the view of Tissot's followers the causes of onanism included lazing around in one's leisure time, spicy food, stimulating drinks, getting up too early and retiring too early, over-strong meat, sausages, certain herbs, full-bodied wine, liqueurs, oysters, mussels, lobster, over-soft beds and tight-fitting woollen clothes. In addition it was stressed that a sexually mature man would only resort to onanism if 'intercourse with the other sex was excluded'. 'Despite the possibility of sexual intercourse', observed one contemporary in 1799, the only men who masturbate are those who fear scandal, feel unable to perform sexual intercourse, or else are afraid of infectious diseases.'

That fact that married men also masturbated was mentioned by various doctors. One psychiatrist quotes the case of a clergyman he knew, father of five children, who continued jerking off energetically. Various writers pointed out that mutual masturbation was performed systematically, quite simply out of fear of pregnancy, couples being forced into it by poverty. There were also accounts of abuse by schoolteachers, seduction by housemaids, stubborn parents who made their sons and daughters sleep in the same bed for too long, while visits to museums, theatres and the ballet 'could excite the child's mind prematurely'. Looking at all kinds of lewd pictures was considered much more harmful.

The causes of masturbation in women were put under the same common denominator as in men: a neuropathological disposition, seduction, haemorrhoids, poor personal hygiene, etc. The consequences included red, irritated labia, leukorrhea, vaginismus, itch and irritation of the womb. If masturbation led to 'neurasthenia sexualis', it resulted in paralysis of the bladder, neurosis of the ovaries, weakness in the legs and ultimately the inability to achieve orgasm. Years of masturbation could also lead to hypersensitivity.

> Female sufferers all described their condition as torment, constant restlessness and pressure in the genitalia. All kinds of sensations (burning, heat, palpitations, agitation, trembling, tickling sensation, squirming, undulating, pressing, pushing, etc.) accompany the condition and the ensuing arousal tempts them to coitus or masturbation, though the act of ejaculation is not one of pleasure, but on the contrary one of revulsion or pain and usually the ailments increase subsequently, like after the very frequently occurring instances of self-pollution.

In the nineteenth century doctors believed that masturbation could result from, for example, eczema of the foreskin, an over-taut foreskin, accumulated smegma and roundworms. The latter worms, which lived in the small intestine, were supposed to provoke masturbation through the itching they caused.

Nursemaids and midwives knew the fairly simple remedy: a piece of bacon attached to a thread was inserted into the child's anus with the objective of luring the roundworms out! With seat worms – which are still around today – exactly the same procedure was followed.

A number of celebrated clinicians have made pronouncements about masturbation over the years, especially among girls. The Danish paediatrician Hirschsprung (1830–1916) – a disorder of the large intestine is named after him – was convinced that masturbation was more prevalent among girls than boys. He reported having seen various young girls masturbating from the age of five months, mostly using rocking movements. Dr Fournier – after whom gangrene of the penis is named – records the case of a girl 'who at the age of four had the genitalia of a fourteen-year-old and masturbated continually, until she died of consumption'. His colleague Ploss mentions some forty cases of masturbating girls: 'In only a few of the cases cited was there, at the age of eight and nine, strong desire for sexual intercourse with men. In one case a girl aged eight miscarried a foetus at two and a half months.' Yet another top authority describes the fate of two girls aged seventeen and twelve: 'Whenever they masturbated, which they did several times a day, they had convulsions and let out appalling screams. Both died a few years later of a psychological disturbance brought on by the evil habit.'

Once upon a time . . .

The German doctor Otto Adler conducted an extensive study of an intelligent 30-year-old woman who had started masturbating at the age of twenty. She did it at intervals of a few weeks. According to Adler she had a need for sexual gratification under the following circumstances: spontaneously immediately before or after menstruation, as a way of curing insomnia, after washing her genitalia, after erotic dreams and sometimes suddenly without any particular reason. He wrote a detailed report:

It took place only in the evenings or at night, and required a particular position, with the right knee bent and the right foot resting against the knee of the extended left leg. Then the index and middle finger were placed firmly on the last third of the left labium minorum, which was rubbed against the parts below. At this point the actions sometimes ceased, either through an attempt at self-control or because the arm had become tired. There was no emission of mucus, or ordinary transpiration, but there was a degree of satisfaction, followed by sleep. However, if the touching was continued, the second stage was reached, and the middle finger entered the vagina, while the index finger remained on the labium and the rest of the hand grasped the whole vulva and squeezed it, from the pubic area to the anus, against the junction of the two pubic bones, with a backwards and forwards movement, with the left hand also being frequently used to support and assist the right. The parts concerned then reacted like mushrooms to the touch, and after a few seconds or a longer interval, the complete sensation of agreeable satisfaction was achieved. At the same moment there was an involuntary raising of the pelvis, together with the emission of mucus, which made the hand wet. This mucus had a smell and was quite different from the usual odourless mucus secreted by the vagina. The finger in the vagina also felt slight contractions in the whole vaginal wall. The climax of sexual pleasure lasted for a few seconds with the accompanying contractions of the vagina, and she was bathed in perspiration and fell asleep almost immediately; if this did not happen, she was often aware of a certain sensitivity in the sacrum, which persisted for several hours, and was most noticeable when sitting down. If masturbation was the result of an erotic dream (which happened quite frequently) the first stage was reached while she was asleep and the second was achieved quicker. While she was engaged in the act her thoughts were only occasionally focused on men or on coitus, since she was concentrating on the climax. Her psychological state afterwards was usually one of self-reproach . . .

Various doctors pointed out that travelling by train could lead to sexual arousal through the vibrations. The sewing machine also came to be seen in an unfavourable light. Older models were heavy and required extensive up and down movements of the legs and the friction could cause sexual arousal in many women. The French medical researcher Theodore Pouillet paid a one-day visit to a factory making military uniforms and reported the following:

Amid the uniform noise, from approximately thirty sewing machines, I suddenly heard one machine going a much higher speed than the rest. I observed the person working at it, a brunette of about eighteen. While automatically making trousers on the machine, her face became animated, her mouth opened slightly, her nostrils flared and her feet began pedalling with increasing speed. Soon I saw a feverish look in her eyes, and her face went pale, her head was thrown back; hands and feet stopped working and stretched out; a muffled cry, followed by a protracted cry was lost in the bustle of the workplace. The girl pulled out her handkerchief in order to wipe the beads of sweat from her brow, and after a shy, embarrassed glance at her workmates she resumed her duties. The supervisor who was acting as my guide and who had seen the direction in which I had been looking, took me over to the girl, who blushed, looked down and muttered a few incoherent words, even before the supervisor had opened her mouth and advised her to sit in the centre of her chair rather than on the edge.

As I was leaving I heard another machine in another part of the room operating at high speed. The supervisor smiled at me and observed that this was such a frequent occurrence that it attracted no attention. It was found particularly, she told me, among young employees, trainees, and those who sat on the edge of their chairs, which greatly facilitated the rubbing of the labia.

The question that arises is what cultural climate existed in Tissot's day. How did the notion of masturbation as a disease with dire consequences ever arise? According to Thomas Laqueur (*Making Sex: Body and Gender from the Greeks to Freud*, 1990) these ideas emerged in an 'economy of plenty' in which people were warned against 'unbounded desire', not only in the form of masturbation, but also embodied by other things that made an 'unbounded' appeal to human imagination, such as reading novels, the use of paper money, etc. Laqueur was to return to this topic in a later book.

Remedies

From the mid-eighteenth century onwards numerous surgical, medical, dietary and behavioural therapies were developed. These included harnesses, metal chastity belts and electrical installations. Another option was to tie the hands to the side of the bed. One British medical journal recommended the placing of a birdcage over the genitals!

In 1818 the surgeon Jalade-Lafond designed a corset for the penis, which reached from the shoulders to the knees. This was followed by other devices, including a metal tube that dangled from a leather jerkin, the brainchild of German Johann Fleck. The German version was perfected by a British invention: a second tube was added for urinating. To protect boys from having erections and masturbating rings were sometimes put over the penis.

Similar equipment had previously been designed for breeding stallions. Horse-breeders had always known that stallions tend to masturbate instead of waiting for a willing mare. This was long before the time when deep-frozen sperm could be stored in sperm banks. Since excessive masturbation has a detrimental effect on the quality of sperm, a kind of net was hung around the penis and an erection caused a bell to ring, so that the horse-breeder could take the necessary action. The devices sold well, at eight dollars each, a considerable sum for the later nineteenth century.

In 1849 a Dr Demeaux made an urgent request to the French Ministry of Education, requiring among other things that dormitories in boarding schools should be so designed that beds were divided into a foot end, which took up two-thirds of the bed, and a head end. The two parts must be divided by a partition, and in this way the foot end of up to a hundred beds could be monitored at night for suspicious movements and the head end could be blacked out by the partition. In addition he proposed trousers without pockets, and finally insisted on unannounced physical examinations of the boys several times a year, on the grounds that masturbators would be apparent to the doctors through the development of their penis. In view of their poor health, they must be specially monitored. Two of the three proposals were rejected, namely the partitioning of beds, on the grounds that such immobility might harm the children, and physical examination, which it was argued might cause acute embarrassment to the stark naked children. The third proposal, the abolition of trouser pockets, had already become common practice.

Extremist religious beliefs provided fertile ground for the acceptance of destructive surgical procedures. These included not only circumcision and castration, but also *infibulation*, or 'sewing shut'. A fibula was originally a pin of bone used by prominent Romans to secure their togas, and the inventor of the procedure was the Roman physician Celsus. In Europe the German Johann Christoph Jaeger (1740–1816) became the principal promoter. Infibulation was practised in the United States from 1860 onwards. It was used in the first place on psychiatric patients, mostly without anaesthetic in order to combine treatment with punishment. It was believed that masturbation was a demonstrable cause of insanity. Castration was also used. In 1856 Luther V. Bell (1806–1862), a leading American psychiatrist and one of the founders of the medical association for the supervision of psychiatric institutions, described the case of a hopeless masturbator who, after the cutting off by ligature of the blood supply to his testicles, recovered and lived an active life.

In his account of a visit to American insane asylums the Scottish doctor Alexander Robertson reported that Dr Wilson Lockhart (1825–1910), director of the Indiana Hospital for the Insane, had developed a way of passing a silver ring through the foreskin in order to prevent masturbation. Unfortunately it was found that the rings occasionally tore free, which required follow-up treatment and the administering of potassium bromide to check sexual urges. Dr Lockhart was a distinguished doctor who in 1866 actually became president of the Indiana State Medical Association. Another American proponent of infibulation was the German-born Abraham Jacobi (1830–1919), a renowned paediatrician. Jacobi's treatment was even more extreme. Especially in the case of young masturbating children he recommended infibulation in combination with the deliberate scarring of the head of the penis in order to provoke a chronic ulcer. Glasgow-based Dr David Yellowlees (1837–1921) developed a special technique based on his unshakable conviction that the foreskin was crucial to the erection of the penis. He reasoned that its physiological role was to continue to cover the engorged penis, and proposed the following surgical treatment:

> the prepuce is drawn well forward, the left forefinger inserted within it down to the root of the glans, and nickel-plated safety pin, introduced from the outside through the skin and mucous membrane, is passed horizontally for half an inch or so past the tip of the left finger, and then brought out through mucous membrane and skin so as to fasten outside. Another pin is similarly fixed on the opposite side of the prepuce. With the

foreskin thus looped, any attempt at erection causes a painful dragging on the pins, and masturbation is effectually prevented. After about a week there will be some ulceration of the mucous membrane with all greater movement and with less pain, when the pins can, if needful, be introduced into a fresh place, but the patient is already convinced that masturbation is not necessary to his existence, and a moral as well as a material victory has been gained.

In the USA Louis Bauer (1814–1898), a German immigrant based in St Louis, also used infibulation to cure both masturbation and epilepsy. The erudite Bauer misused quotations from Celsus, Martial and Juvenal to justify the use of infibulation in combating masturbation. In rather clumsy jargon he describes the technique used in his first case, a 22-year-old man, as follows: 'I perforated the prepuce by a trocar on two opposite places, introduced through the wounds two sounds, No. 2, and twisted them together like rings.' The result of the procedure was usually an extensive painful swelling for at least two months, which according to Bauer could ensure that the patient did not revert to his bad habits. His second case was another 22-year-old man. This time Bauer dispensed with the silver rings: 'I transfixed the prepuce by two silk slings and directed to fasten them in front of the glans penis on going to bed, the object of the infibulations being to wake the patient by pain when the penis should get in a state of erection.'

The principal object of the operation was to prevent nocturnal emissions, since Bauer and most of his contemporaries were convinced that these caused epilepsy. Anxious parents in search of information in order to monitor masturbation as in their children had a large number of books to choose from. One of them, *Plain Facts for Old and Young* (1888) had been written by the popular and influential surgeon John Harvey Kellogg (1853–1943), co-founder of the cornflakes empire. Its basic message was that based on experience of the treatment of masturbation in the mentally handicapped, the preferred solution was to secure the foreskin with silver wire over the head of the penis, which rendered erection impossible. Neither Kellogg nor any other advocates of infibulation discussed the problems resulting from 'pinning closed', including of course difficulties with urinating as well as personal hygiene.

By the end of the First World War infibulation was a thing of the past in Europe: doctors had better ways to spend their time than promote sexual repression. The war had created new health crises, and in addition medical discoveries had demonstrated that many ailments formerly attributed to masturbation were the result of 'real' diseases, including tuberculosis. Other infectious diseases were discovered, which in many cases could be adequately treated. In the USA the reason for the phasing out of infibulation was the routine circumcision of male infants. The procedure was carried out in maternity hospitals, usually on the first or second day after birth and without anaesthetic. All kinds of clamps were developed to simplify the procedure. The idea was that it would not only prevent masturbation, but would also combat sexually transmitted diseases or sexual neurasthenia, urinary tract infections and cervical cancer.

Neurasthenia, nutrition and more curious objects

The British were responsible for naming the new diseases: spermatorrhoea or sexual neurasthenia. The previously mentioned English sexologist Havelock Ellis observed that the only solution for a highly sexed young man was to enter a monastery, and devoted forty pages to the subject.

At the end of the nineteenth century doctors believed that masturbation, the spilling of one's seed, led not only to impotence but to general debilitation. A doctor of the period wrote:

The masturbator cannot perform intercourse, his member having lost its resilience, its capacity for erection. The noble liquid, his strength, his maleness, his beauty have been lost. The source from which energy, mental power, courage and pride, talent and pleasure sprang, has dried up, has been recklessly spilled; perhaps something is left, but the little that remains is thin, watery, feeble and what is more flows away too fast.

William Alexander Hammond (1828–1900), a surgeon and later professor of nervous and mental diseases in New York, was convinced that masturbation, particularly at an early age, was the principal reason for the later absence of an erection.

In the second chapter of his book *Sexual Impotence in the Male and Female* (1887) Hammond takes over a hundred pages to set out his view of things. Organs must be 'mature' before they can be subjected to stress. If a child is compelled to study at too young

Victims of masturbation.

an age, it runs a serious risk of contracting epilepsy or becoming a dunce. Excessive manual work will stunt the child's growth and make it backward and weak. Hammond is therefore convinced that stimulating the sex organs at too young an age will lead to impotence:

> In very young infants it is sometimes the case that in order to soothe them nurses titillate the genital organs and thus produce sensations which are agreeable and which are subsequently desired. Eventually, the operation is performed by the child, and, being continued through the period of puberty, leads to complete impotence from loss of power, and often from loss of desire also.

As a warning the professor tells the story of a young shepherd who takes to masturbation from an early age by inserting twigs into his urethra. Eventually the practice leads to horrific complications, which are still occasionally found, in a less serious form, in modern urinary medicine.

The self-styled Professor Jacobus Schoondermark (1849–1915), a prolific popular medical writer, summarizes the extensive literature on tactile stimulation in masturbation in a work of 1902, which discusses auto-eroticism and mutual masturbation in children and adults of both sexes, its consequences and treatment. Among the examples quoted is a primary schoolteacher who masturbated with a bent length of steel wire, until the wire became caught in a fold of membrane, necessitating an operation. Another doctor mentions a 50-year-old man who masturbated with a darning needle until the tip broke and found its way into the front section of his bladder. Dr Kreps from St Petersburg reports the case of 'a young man, who appeared regularly at the surgery, ostensibly to have thick catheters inserted into his urethra because of sexual neurasthenia, but in reality to have himself masturbated by the doctor'.

Naturally there is a catalogue of anecdotes on wedding bands and brass curtain rings, and the French surgeon François Chopart (1743–1795) even produced an anthology of objects used in masturbation. He also described the vicissitudes of a shepherd, Gabriel Galien,

> who had engaged in auto-eroticism from the age of fifteen with such frenzy that he would masturbate up to eight times a day. After some time ejaculations became scarcer and required such an effort that he had to labour for an hour to achieve one, reducing him to a state of complete convulsion, and producing only a few drops of blood and no sperm. Up to the age of twenty-six he used only his hand to satisfy his fateful urges. Subsequently, when he could no longer achieve ejaculation by this means, which simply kept his penis in a virtually constant state of erection, he hit upon the idea of stimulating his urethra with a thin wooden stick about six inches long. He inserted it quite deeply, without applying any grease or mucus as a lubricant, which might have alleviated somewhat the acute pressure exerted on such a sensitive organ. His chosen occupation of shepherd often enabled him to be alone and hence to indulge his inclinations at his leisure; hence he repeatedly spent several hours a day stimulating his urethra with his stick. He used it constantly for sixteen years, and was able to achieve more or less copious ejaculations. As a result of this repeated and lengthy friction, the urethra became hard, calloused and completely insensitive. Now, finding his stick as useless as his hand, Galien considered himself the unhappiest of mortals. The insurmountable aversion to women, his forced abstinence, the constant erections that aroused him and his inability to find relief, did indeed seemed to justify that idea. In that state of melancholy oppression, which affected him both physically and morally, our shepherd often allowed his flock to stray, obsessed as he was with finding a way of achieving satisfaction.

After numerous experiments, all unsuccessful, he returned to the stick with renewed frenzy; but realising in despair that this only stimulated his misguided desires, he took a rough knife out of his pocket and made an incision along the whole length of the urethral canal. This incision, which would have caused anyone else the severest pain, caused him only a pleasurable sensation, followed by a full ejaculation. Excited by this fortunate discovery, he resolved to make up for his forced abstinence whenever the frenzy seized him. Ditches, woods, and rocks served as hiding places where he could indulge in or repeat this new activity, which unfailingly provided him with the pleasure and ejaculation he expected. After having given full rein to his urges, he reached the point, after perhaps a thousand repetitions, where he had cut his penis into two separate halves, from the head of that section of the urethra and the erectile tissue as far as the scrotum and the pubic bone joint. If there was heavy bleeding, he would staunch it by tightening a band around the penis until the bleeding stopped. After three or four hours he removed the tourniquet and left the severed parts as they were. The various incisions made in his penis in no way dampened his ardour. The sections of erectile tissue, although severed, often became erect, branching left and right.

These stories may lead you to think that masturbation with strange objects no longer occurs nowadays. In fact every urologist knows of a patient who has sought sexual gratification in solitude with the aid of an electric cable or something similar. However, such experiments usually wind up in a chilly operating theatre, when the cable has started twisting in the urethra.

The use of vacuum cleaners is equally notorious. In Florida a case with fatal consequences was reported. The 57-year-old man in question was discovered when his neighbour became annoyed at the continuous noise of a vacuum cleaner. The forensic pathologists

Imami and Kemal described the gruesome details. The man had ligatured his testicles with a pair of panties. Since no sperm was found it was suspected that the man had not succeeded in achieving orgasm; he had first tried to come by penetrating himself anally with a wooden table leg. When questioned, his wife said that she had previously caught him in the act with a vacuum cleaner, and added that she had refused to have sex with him for the last five years.

An extremely strange form of masturbation was reported some years ago in a specialist urological journal. A 40-year-old man attended the Accident and Emergency department of a hospital in Pennsylvania. His scrotum was the size of a grapefruit; the left side had been torn open and the testicle was missing. The patient said that he had been injured at work a few days earlier. After further questioning he admitted that he had got into the habit at work of holding his erect penis against the canvas drive wheel of a conveyor belt, while his colleagues were at lunch. One day, when he was on the point of ejaculating, his scrotum was caught between the pulley and the belt. The man had closed the wound with eight staples from a staple gun and had gone cheerfully back to work!

In the USA there was a remarkable link between nutrition and masturbation. Both Sylvester Graham, the inventor of the cracker, and John Harvey Kellogg, the previously mentioned cornflake magnate, came up with a diet-based solution. In Graham's eyes each ejaculation was equivalent to a considerable loss of blood. Kellogg maintained that masturbation was even worse than sodomy, that is, homosexuality.

Inventors looked for new devices to prevent self-abuse. The penis corset of 1818 had proved too restrictive. Between 1856 and 1932 the American authorities granted 33 patents. The US Patent Office even patented an alarm that went off in the parents' bedroom if their child's bed began moving in a suspicious way. Meanwhile in Europe all kinds of pills, syrups and beverages were developed. Examples included pills made of crystallized sulphuric acid and iron, syrup of lactic acid and sugar and drinks containing calcium chloride, magnesium chloride, carbonated soda, table salt, sulphuric acid and iron, sulphuric acid soda and carbonated water.

Dr George Weber of Geneva advertised indirectly in the booklet *Mankind's Secret Ailments*, which is full of letters and testimonials from grateful patients:

> Dear Sir, I am a clerk in a large company. For some time I have been in a weak, nervous state and although I have consulted various specialists about my case and have followed their instructions closely, I have found it impossible to regain my health. On the contrary, I am in a worse state than at the beginning. But after reading your excellent book, I believe I have at last found someone who can release me from my suffering.
>
> Like many others I have weakened my originally strong constitution through masturbation. I must have been about twelve when I was first introduced to the practice by a school-mate, and I continued in the habit for many years. Until about three years ago I had not the slightest suspicion that so many terrible spinal ailments were attributable to it. Afterwards I made serious efforts to break the habit. Sadly, this did not restore me to good health . . .

After describing his physical state the patient continues:

> But that is not all. My memory has also been badly affected. My self-confidence has gone and I feel so depressed that I can think of nothing except my own condition and the thought that the phenomena now manifesting themselves may herald a more serious disease, drives me almost to despair. When that happens I lose all my mental strength, shut myself up in my house and avoid all company . . .

I am moderate in my habits, and do not smoke or drink excessively. I limit myself to one pipe after each meal, and no more than two in the evening. I take as much exercise as possible, but my work is sedentary.

Now that I have told you my whole history, I look forward eagerly to your advice and the medications you prescribe. If you succeed in curing me I shall be eternally grateful. I should like you to send the necessary medication by return, and enclose an initial payment of two guineas, so you can begin treatment without delay . . .

Dr Weber describes the outcome:

This young man underwent treatment for slightly less than three months, during which time there was a fairly intensive correspondence. Since the patient had followed all instructions faithfully, by the end of the treatment he was not only completely cured of his affliction, but also considerably strengthened in mind and body.

In all cases where the patient lives a long distance away, it is advisable to send payment in advance so that treatment can begin immediately. In this way we treat on a daily basis patients from all parts of Europe, Africa, North and South America, the Indies and Japan, and even Australia.

Ultimately neither the engineers with their devices, the doctors with their potions, their forced sterilizations, circumcisions and committals to lunatic asylums, nor the priests of all denominations could stem the tide.

Clitoridectomy

The treatment of masturbation through surgery reached its apogee with patients who had 'only' a clitoris. According to the general medical wisdom of the late nineteenth century it made no difference to a woman's feelings whether she had genitalia or not. Although the doctors, all of them men, had been unable to convince either themselves or the public that penis amputation was the preferred treatment for masturbation, they were able to deal with women by advocating removal of the clitoris, or *clitoridectomy*. A number of doctors were later to opt for cauterization rather than excision.

Viennese professor Gustav Braun recommended the procedure in his *Compendium der Frauenkrankheiten* (1863). In Britain the operation was introduced by Isaac Baker-Brown, a prominent surgeon and gynaecologist, and later a highly respected president of the Medical Society. He considered the operation advisable, since he believed that masturbation in women led to hysteria, epilepsy and varicose veins. For him it was an obvious step to cure masturbation by removal of the organ associated with sexual pleasure. He performed the operation with great frequency on both girls and women and had set up a special clinic called the 'London Surgical Home', where in 1866 he 'treated' 48 children.

In 1882 the French medical journal for nervous and psychiatric disorders *L'Encéphale* published a lengthy article by an Istanbul-based doctor Demetrius Alexandre Zambaco on 'Masturbation and Mental Illness in Two Young Girls'. The elder of the two masturbated constantly. There was no other option but to remove the clitoris, Dr Zambaco explains:

It is undeniable that cauterising with a red-hot iron reduces the sensitivity of the clitoris and that after repeated cauterizations it is possible to remove it completely. Understandably, children, after they have lost sensitivity as a result of treatment, are less easily stimulated and less inclined to touch themselves . . .

Zambaco then states that he has met a number of internationally renowned colleagues, among them Dr Jules Guérin of London, who had achieved excellent results by removing the clitoris through cauterization. Such operations were not stopped until 1905, mainly due to the protests of Sigmund Freud against this kind of mutilation in his *Three Essays on the Theory of Sexuality*.

The 'Bringers of Enlightenment'

For several centuries masturbation was considered as a 'sinful affliction'. In his *Solitary Sex: A Cultural History of Masturbation* (2003) the American historian Thomas W. Laqueur shows that the foundations for the taboo on masturbation were laid not by the Church, but by the progressive thinkers of the Enlightenment. When he told colleagues that he was researching the history of the perception of masturbation, he encountered furtive sniggers and sceptical comments such as 'keep a cool head, or you'll never finish the book'. These reactions confirmed the historian's conviction that his project was necessary.

For eighteen months Laqueur immersed himself in the study of diaries, autobiographies, works of art, literature, pornography, websites and official documents. He demonstrates that rigid attitudes to the subject can be traced directly back to the Enlightenment. He calls turning masturbation into a problem the dark side of the period in which the modern world is rooted: parallel with the rise of reason and science and the awakening of autonomous individualism, masturbation was branded as a dangerous, sinful, egotistical act. In all preceding periods – in antiquity, in Judaic and Christian culture – it was matter scarcely worth attention, a humble, rather obscure activity to which no ponderous moral judgement was attached.

With striking precision the historian identifies the essence of the great fear with which people have for centuries have secretly indulged in auto-eroticism: in around 1712 the British surgeon John Marten, in a treatise entitled *Onania, or the Heinous Sin of*

Self Pollution (inspired by the Old Testament figure of Onan, punished for choosing to pour his seed on the ground rather than father a child with his late brother's wife), describes 'onanism' as a new disease. Marten explains that masturbation is widespread and frequently practised out of sheer ignorance: 'Through solitude or vanity boys learn self-abuse and self-pollution, without knowing how wrong and dangerous it really is.'

His treatise became a veritable sensation, and sold widely. Published in medical journals and ordinary newspapers it found its way all round Europe.

One of Laqueur's discoveries is that Marten may have derived his notions from a Dutchman. As early as 1698 a Latin treatise on vice by one Hadriaan Beverland (1650–1716) had appeared in England, in which thirty pages were devoted to masturbation. It attracted little or no attention and remained on the shelf. It was not translated and the book is nowhere quoted in the eighteenth and nineteenth-century literature. Even Tissot, who spent his whole life in search of allies, probably never saw a copy.

Like John Marten, Beverland was a shadowy figure, a philologist, lawyer and freethinker in the tradition of Spinoza. He was probably born in Antwerp but grew up in Middelburg, and studied law successively in Franeker (1668), Leiden (where he matriculated in 1673), Franeker again (1676) and Utrecht (1677). Having been brought up in the humanist tradition he was first and foremost a philologist with a special interest in Latin erotic literature. His most important work is *De peccato originali*, which appeared anonymously in 1678, and which argues that the Bible should be interpreted allegorically. A second edition was published in 1679 under the author's own name. This resulted in Beverland's arrest in Leiden in the same year, the imposition of a fine and banishment from Holland and Zeeland. He went to Oxford, where he resumed his studies and wrote satirical pieces about local clergy, which provoked resentment. It is possible that he wrote his Latin book on vice there, since in the Netherlands he had already had very unpleasant experiences after publishing a book suggesting that the sin of Adam and Eve was sexual in nature. That had been publicly burned. Even after freedom of religion was introduced in the seventeenth century Spinoza too preferred to write his works on religion in Latin, in the hope that strict Calvinists would be unable to read him. Beverland died virtually insane in very poor circumstances in London.

Back to Dr Marten. Thomas Laqueur reveals that Marten, like many of his colleagues, did not act completely without self-interest, and in fact placed advertisements for all kinds of medicines, such as vaginal drops, penis ointments and powders, all designed to curb solitary sexual gratification, in the same papers in which his article on the 'new' disease appeared. In Laqueur's view the great success of both his moral condemnation and the sales of his cures – he created his own pharmaceutical industry – made Marten the originator of the taboo. In his wake progressive philosophers like Kant and Rousseau adopted the same vision: masturbation did not fit into the new image of man as a rational, social being who had to keep his own desires and urges completely under control. Masturbation sprang from the imagination and bore no relation to reality, and made people susceptible to addiction. Laqueur describes it as 'the crack cocaine of sexuality'.

Why did all this fall on such fertile ground? Was it because of the medical view current at the time that the body was an energy field that was thrown off balance by the discharge of juices? Or was it linked to a deeper fear of a complete loss of self-control associated with death? Thomas Laqueur shows that the morality of emergent medical science usurped the latent medieval religious aversion to 'luxury'. The Church also considered the experience of sexual pleasure and specifically the committing of an act not aimed at reproduction, a form of depraved vanity, non-productive recreation and idleness.

Laqueur, who as befits a historian is not fond of the psychological approach, sets the emergence of masturbation as a problem

partly in the context of the fear of rapid urbanization in eighteenth-century France. He believes that during the transition from
an agrarian to an industrial society people were afraid of a loss of
fertility. People believed that if they indulged in masturbation they
would no longer be able perform their duty to work and marry –
and without the family France would collapse.

For centuries the commandment 'thou shalt not masturbate',
which became a paradoxical fusion between the progressive spirit
of the Enlightenment and conservative ecclesiastical views, held
the community morally in its thrall. Far into the twentieth century
masturbating patients were informed of the gruesome consequences of their behaviour: mutilation, blindness, hysteria, aggres-
sion and madness (particularly in women), kidney disorders or a
deformed spine, the familiar endless litany. This pathology
sparked a new industry, supplying products like erection alarm
apparatuses, penis sheaths and for girls special gloves and band-
ages to prevent them from opening their legs.

The fact that knowledge did not prevent people from continuing to masturbate indicates that moral crusaders have little or
no influence over human actions. Possibly prohibition actually
gave a stimulus to the precursors of today's porn industry, since
the denunciation of the sin on an ever-wider scale was paralleled
by a lively trade in prints showing men and women in states of
solitary, blissful sensual abandon.

Scholars in the humanities

With the advent of psychiatry at the end of the nineteenth century the subject of masturbation passed into the realm of the
humanities. The two greatest contributions to this development
are those of Richard von Krafft-Ebing and Sigmund Freud.

Krafft-Ebing (1840–1902) was a psychiatrist whose enduring
fame rests on his magnum opus *Psychopathia Sexualis*. The first
edition of the book appeared in 1886 and was an immediate hit:

the motto 'sex sells' applied even then. Despite the fact that the writer deliberately used Latin words to strip stormier passages of their erotic charge, the book was avidly read. Interestingly, though, it was 1965 before an unbowdlerized edition appeared. All in all, the book is full of errors, which are presented fairly pretentiously as if they were the fruit of solid scholarly research. For example, without a shred of scientific evidence the author states that sexual aberrations are based mainly on hereditary disorders of the nervous system.

Krafft-Ebing's lugubrious case histories reinforce the impression that he was mainly concerned to separate sick, sordid, perverted individuals from healthy, wholesome people with controlled sex lives geared to procreation. The titles of these case studies speak volumes: 'Exhibitionist', 'Pictures and Self-Pollution', 'The Women-Haters' Ball', 'Necrophilia', 'Rape and Sex Murder'. He expressed his view of masturbation as follows:

> This practice robs the burgeoning bud of its perfume and its beauty, leaving only the crude animal urge to sexual gratification. The glow of sensual sensitivity is snuffed out and the inclination towards the opposite sex is weakened.

The founder of modern sexology does not go much further than his colleagues from the early nineteenth century. Sigmund Freud, the founding father of psychoanalysis, is considered a sexual revolutionary. While not regarding masturbation as normal, he did see it as a useful phase on the way to adulthood. Through masturbation young people could 'dispense with their father-figure'. In 1898, however, he stated that 'if masturbation causes neurosis' (a popular diagnosis at the time) the prevention of the practice deserves more attention than it has hitherto received'.

The importance that Freud and his colleagues from the early days attached to masturbation is clear from the fact that between 1908 and 1912 thirteen meetings of the Vienna Psychoanalytic

Society were devoted to discussion of the topic. The minutes show that the idea that masturbation led to neurosis was soon elevated into a dogma. At the end of these deliberations Freud concluded that masturbation led to 'neurosis' and possibly even 'organic' damage. Even more absurdly, Freud labelled all kinds of non-genital activity as masturbation. In *The Unconscious* (1915), for example, he quotes the case of a young man who was fond of squeezing his spots (he was covered in them, so no wonder . . .). For Freud, however, the squeezing was a substitute for masturbation, and the cavity created was the female sex organ. In Freud's view this represented a realization of the threat of castration. Well . . .

However much psychoanalysts presented themselves as liberal, they were generally rather opposed to women's right to structure their sexual lives for themselves. Wasn't it Freud himself who labelled the clitoral orgasm as 'infantile' and the vaginal orgasm as 'adult'? Obviously the idea that adult women could reach orgasm without a penetrative phallus was not congenial to him. As late as 1973 an article appeared in the principal journal of American psychologists entitled 'On a Special Type of Masturbation in Women: Masturbation with Water'. The author, one Halpert, tried to find an answer to the question of why some women chose this particular solution to their subconscious dilemmas. The answer was obvious: women who masturbate by letting water run over their clitoris did so in order to express an associated fantasy, namely 'I have my father's phallus and can urinate and ejaculate like a man and with those powerful streams I can destroy and castrate in revenge for the castration that has been carried out on me.' From all this it is clear how for decades after the death of Freud psychiatrists resisted the idea that masturbation is a completely natural phenomenon.

Another telling example was the review of the *Hite Report* (1981) in the *Journal of the American Psychoanalytic Association*. The book's author, Shere Hite, stated plainly that it was not the vagina but the clitoris that was the principal organ of sexual pleasure in women. She linked to that fact a powerful rejection – certainly nothing new – of men's tendency to establish norms for female sexuality. Hite's insistence that women had just as much right as men to define their own sexuality drew unpleasant comments from the reviewer (a psychiatrist). Or did he believe that only Freud was entitled to tell women how to have sex?

After the Second World War the United States produced some enlightened researchers. Dr Alfred Kinsey saw large-scale surveys of the sexual habits of his countrymen as a possible solution. He hoped that this would refute all kinds of prejudices. He amassed the second largest collection of written material on sex; the Vatican will most probably remain in first place until the end of time. Kinsey is runner-up with over 8,000 case histories. In 1953 this likeable, soft-voiced academic with a predilection for bow ties, whose previous professional experience with the opposite sex had been confined to the sexuality of female gall wasps, published the first opinion survey of the sexuality of the average man and woman, including masturbation. Eighty-eight per cent of respondents in the 16–20 age group were found to indulge in masturbation. Because they revealed a great deal – too much – about American sex life and gave sexuality a scientific status, Kinsey's findings were mercilessly pilloried, especially by politicians, and he died a broken man a few years later.

It was no wonder that it was the mid-1960s before Masters and Johnson came forward to further advance the cause of sexology. They were advocates of masturbation, since they believed that it had a salutary effect both on the marital relationship and on general health. As regards marital relations, they maintained that it would be sensible for half of married Americans to masturbate, given their sexual incompetence, which threatened their marital happiness. From a medical point of view it was, Masters and Johnson believed, of particular value to women and elderly men. Women should masturbate, they argued, because it improved the blood flow during menstruation and alleviated abdominal cramps and back pain. Elderly men should masturbate in order to stay in shape sexually. Under the motto of 'use it or lose it', the researchers prescribed a kind of jogging for the penis.

In fact Masters and Johnson stuck to the old doctrine of masturbation. That became crystal clear when they believed they had discovered a new sexological disease, namely 'situational anorgasmia in masturbation'. So what was it? Well, for its discoverers it was a 'real' disease, almost always caused by religion. The 'sick' women were unable to achieve orgasm when masturbating. Masters and Johnson identified the subjects in whom it occurred (as expected, only in women) and reported on their treatment of eleven patients, of whom ten recovered. However, it was clear from their description of the pathology of the cases in question that they were simply pulling the wool over the eyes of their gullible readers and followers: women unable to achieve orgasm through masturbation, they argued, would never have climaxed as a result of masturbation or manipulation during homosexual or heterosexual sex play, but would achieve orgasm through coitus.

In retrospect their new sexological disease contained an implicit insult. In whatever human situation a woman achieved orgasm in any other way than through coitus (homosexual, heterosexual, or alone, lovingly or lovelessly, etc.), and via whatever method she achieved it (by hand, an artificial penis, a vibrator, with the showerhead, etc.), for Masters and Johnson such an orgasm constituted proof that the woman was orgasmic when masturbating. That was their euphemism for healthy, normal, good. As a result they concluded that women who were able to achieve orgasm in heterosexual coitus, but not through masturbation, were suffering from 'anorgasmia in masturbation', their euphemism for sick, abnormal and hence bad.

The discovery of this disease was nothing more than a reversal of the old doctrine that masturbation could make you mad. In the nineteenth century masturbation was a disease and abstinence from masturbation the treatment, while Masters and Johnson saw non-masturbation as a disease and masturbation as the treatment!

Shere Hite also wrote about male sexuality. Among her findings was the fact that many men feel guilty while masturbating, but at the same time enjoy it greatly. The sexual revolution and feminism freed the experience of pleasure from guilt feelings and anxiety. In the context of the notion that sex could (if not must) be pleasurable, masturbation acquired the position of ultimate self-discovery.

Nowadays doctors have lost all interest in masturbation. Entering the word 'masturbation' in PubMed – *the* scientific source for the medical world – produces less than 2,000 hits, while Google provides over 90 million.

Masturbation and prostate cancer

Over the years various studies have been conducted into a possible link between the frequency of ejaculation and the risk of both benign enlargement and cancer of the prostate. This would make the celebrated rock musician Frank Zappa (1940–1993) turn in his grave. Zappa, who died of an aggressive form of prostate cancer, sang the praises of masturbation in several of his songs. He was an unconventional figure and in 1985 took part in a public hearing organized by the Parents' Music Resource Center (PMC), whose members included Tipper Gore, the wife of Al Gore. This body maintained that the American record industry was exposing the youth of America to 'sex, violence and the glorification of drugs and alcohol'. Zappa acted as the champion of musical freedom and passionately contested the views of the PMRC. With biting wit Frank Zappa exposes the hypocrisy of puritan America. In tribute to his memory let us briefly list his arguments:

There is no conclusive scientific proof for the assertion that exposure to any kind of music will lead the listener to commit a crime, or send his soul to hell.

Masturbation is not illegal. If the activity is not illegal, why should it be illegal to sing about it?

There is no medical evidence for linking hairy palms, warts or blindness to masturbation or vaginal arousal, just as there is no evidence that listening to references to either of these two subjects automatically changes the listener into an unstable social being.

The ratification of legislation against masturbation could be a lengthy and costly process.

There are not enough prison cells to lock up all the children who do it.

For the uninitiated: Zappa took musical revenge in the album *FZ Meets the Mothers of Prevention*, 1985.

In the 1980s the theory was regularly advanced that regular ejaculation – through coitus or masturbation – increased the risk of prostate cancer. The idea was that frequent ejaculation caused the prostate to increase in size. In addition men were exposed to all kinds of viruses and bacteria that could somehow lead to prostate cancer. These ideas proved false; indeed, the opposite may be true. In the early 1990s researchers at the American Cancer Institute asked almost 30,000 men (aged between 46 and 81) how often they ejaculated when they turned 20 and 40.

They were also asked how often they ejaculated in 1991, the year the survey was launched. After eight years of follow-up, 1,449 men were found to have developed prostate cancer. The average number of ejaculations per month was between four and seven. Those who ejaculated more often showed no increased risk of cancer. In fact, among the men with the highest number of ejaculations (over 20 a month) a reduced risk was observed. The study was carried out only among white men and of the 30,000 participants relatively few ejaculated very frequently. Of course further research followed. Young men up to the age of 40 were increasing the chance of prostate cancer by masturbating, but in men over 50 masturbation on the contrary had a prophylactic role, wrote British researchers in 2009. The experts asked over 400 men with

prostate cancer, all aged 50 and above, how often they had masturbated or made love in various periods of their life, and put the
same question to 400 healthy contemporaries. Sexual intercourse
turned out to have no bearing on the risk of prostate cancer, but
masturbation did. Men who had masturbated in their twenties
(between twice and seven times a week) were almost twice as likely
to suffer from prostate cancer as those who had masturbated once
a month at most. The same applied to fanatics in their thirties.
With 40-year-olds the link suddenly disappeared, and with 50-
year-olds the reverse applied: the risk was 30 per cent less if they
had masturbated frequently. At their advanced age 'frequently'
meant more than once a week.

There were immediate derisive responses on the internet.
'Does that prostate cancer come before or after blindness?' someone wondered. Someone else had no confidence in the test subjects. 'Only three out of ten men said that they had masturbated
frequently in their twenties. That means all the rest were lying, or
had their hands in plaster for an extended period.' I had immediate doubts about the frequencies reported. The test subjects pur-
ported to have a very clear memory of their sex life, even going
back decades. That struck me as implausible. What is more, the
researchers had not checked if the healthy 50-year-olds were in
fact free of cancer. Very careless, since three out of ten men over
50 have prostate cancer without knowing it. In short: was the comparison fair?

It is also worth mentioning that in 2003 a comparable study
had appeared in the same *British Journal of Urology*. On that
occasion the conclusion was the opposite: five or more ejaculations a week in their twenties and thirties appeared to protect the
respondents at a later age. No one over 40 participated in the
latter survey.

Another question was: how could masturbation be unhealthy
for younger and healthy for older men? The scientists wrestled
with the problem too: they suspected that horny young men

have an extra large supply of sex hormones that incidentally affect the prostate. In older men, they argued, ejaculations 'rinsed' the prostate clean, washing away accumulated toxins. But, the researchers admitted, one might argue that things were the other way round and older men lost interest because their dormant tumours decreased their sexual pleasure. Who is to say?

In the light of so much uncertainty no one need change his habits. There will probably never be an unambiguous answer. A truly well-founded study requires men in their twenties to be monitored for about 40 years, their testosterone levels to be checked regularly, their sexual behaviour to be mapped and samples of their prostate to be taken. Who would be foolish enough to agree to such a trial? And what urologist can spare the time? There is unlikely ever to be a last judgement on this question.

After removal of the whole prostate and the seminal vesicles (radical prostatectomy) no ejaculate is released at orgasm. Though the rhythmic contractions of the pelvic floor during orgasm persist, the contractions of the seminal vesicles and the prostate can of course no longer be felt. As a result most patients experience a subjective change. The orgasm becomes less intense; the physical sensation may vary from a scarcely perceptible feeling in the region of the pelvic floor to a series of powerful waves through the whole body with aftershocks. The process of ejaculation becomes slower with age, and the sensation of orgasm less powerful.

Since in men who have undergone radical protstatectomy only the external sphincter muscle remains, during orgasm, when the pelvis and the external sphincter alternately contract and relax, there may be, in the absence of any contraflow of ejaculate, some loss of urine. For this reason it is imperative for this group of patients to urinate thoroughly before coitus.

Other modern insights

Modern sexologists see masturbation as a form of sperm quality maintenance. The sperm is never allowed to become old and past its sell-by date. In one of his works the writer Joost Zwagerman describes 'Villa Masturbatia' as a 'spa with no waiting list'. Truman Capote felt the attraction of masturbation was that he didn't have to get dressed up for it, and 50 years ago a popular American academic told his students: 'It saves time and money, you avoid quite a few unpleasant relationships and obligations, it makes no one unhappy and there's no risk of infectious diseases'. The celebrated film-maker Woody Allen hit the nail on the head when he said: I won't hear a bad word about masturbation. It's sex with someone I love!' Or in the words of a well-known Dutch comic duo: 'Simultaneous orgasm guaranteed!'

What these humorists are mostly talking about is the safe, hermetic aesthetics of masturbation by male heterosexuals. Hermetic, because it precludes any intrusion of a soft, vaginal element, a softness that is hard to reconcile with the phallic hardness that the masturbator feels and that drives him on to discharge. The *moment suprême* always arrives on time for the masturbating man; there is no need for any competition in the sense of simultaneous orgasm. This last point places the act of love between man and woman in an alarming light. Willy-nilly, the problem of failure as a lover or even impotence looms. The masturbator is spared any psychological warfare with a woman, the ideal partner who always comes at the same time is his own reflection. So much for modern psychological insights.

When it comes to physiology important research has been carried out in recent decades. Behavioural scientists Brody and Krüger researched the prolactin level in the blood before and after sexual intercourse and also before and after masturbation. The hormone prolactin triggers milk production in mammals, but it has many more functions. It is known, for instance, that at the moment of orgasm there is a huge peak. It produces a feeling of gratification. What did they find? After sexual intercourse the prolactin level was 400 times higher than after masturbation, assuming of course that in both cases orgasm was achieved. From a scientific point of view, therefore, it is better for the emotions to make love than to masturbate, and that applies to both men and women!

The internet and diaries

Since 2005 Jochen Peter (1972), a senior lecturer at the Amsterdam School of Communications, has been researching the effect of internet porn on young people in the Research Centre for Young People and the Media at the University of Amsterdam. When he began his research he was astonished to discover that virtually no reliable research data was available. His first objective was to establish the size of the online sex industry and he found figures that pointed in all directions. Companies are reluctant to divulge their part in the provision of porn. Think of the hotel chains where there is a bible in the bedside table, but where guests have access to a pay-as-you-go adult TV channel.

In one of his studies Peter investigated the frequency with which young people aged between thirteen and eighteen watched porn on the internet. In the six months preceding the survey over 70 per cent of boys and 40 per cent of girls had done so at least once. Keeping sexually explicit material away from children is a difficult job. Anti-porn software can be easily bypassed by smart children. Internet platforms are becoming increasingly portable, and everything can already be watched on a mobile, which is impossible to monitor. This is the great difference from the pre-internet period, when the local tobacconist or video rentals manager stood between the consumer and his porn. It is almost inevitable that the free availability of sexually explicit material will have a marked impact on the sexual morals of the growing internet generation.

'You can't jump to that conclusion,' says Jochen Peter in an interview of June 2009. There are other influences on morality besides porn, he explains. The climate of the times, for example. 'My period of sexual socialization was in the 1980s, when because of AIDS sex was associated with danger. That is much less true now. It is important to know what are the dominant values and how sexual roles are defined, before you can say anything about the impact of porn.'

The results of his four years' research are remarkable. It turns out that those who watch internet porn are less secure and less content with their sex lives. One qualification is that this applies only to young people who have not yet had sex with a partner. 'They think: wow, if that's the standard, I don't come up to the mark,' says the researcher. It was also found that those who make frequent use of porn are more inclined to see women as sex objects. This also has to be qualified: pornography can be both a cause and an effect, since the reverse is equally true: those who regard women as sex objects tend to watch internet pornography more often. In addition this applies to only a minority of boys *and* girls. 'This is one of the mysteries our research has thrown up.'

Another finding was that for young people who watch porn frequently the link between love and sex is less important. They consider sexual experimentation more important and have no problem with sex outside a relationship.

Is sexual behaviour on the internet the innocent modern form of 'sex behind the bike shed'? Yes, said a leading sexologist a few years back, and you shouldn't get too worked up about it. Every generation has its own form of sexual expression. 'But,' he added, 'because of the internet there is now instant sex – anonymous, available twenty-four hours a day, accessible to all. This instant sex has brought sexual fantasies closer. And the internet visualizes everything, making the images more incisive and the arousal more powerful.' It is definitely true that young people are especially prone to cross boundaries on the internet.

It often begins innocently. Cautious feelers are extended towards online communities: social networking sites like Myspace. Then through the chatroom someone builds up a new circle of friends. If they hit it off with someone, they can continue chatting in private, make an actual date or decide to webcam together, for example on MSN. This may result in secretly filmed webcam images of stripping and masturbation, which are then, with or without resort to blackmail, posted on the internet. But even the unsuspecting computer user can fall prey to a hacker, as many well-publicized examples show.

On the internet one can take a look at all kinds of masturbation diaries, which show that there are people for whom it is almost a full-time job. There are also masturbation groups. Let me take the reader to one such anonymous site:

This site is about masturbation, male masturbation, my masturbation. Masturbation is my favourite kind of sex. I believe that it's my sexual orientation, besides being gay. I masturbate daily, sometimes for hours. I like edging a lot. You could call me an Onanist, a Masturbator or whatsoever. I don't care. I consider it a healthy outlet and I do enjoy it. I called this website: Journal of an Onanist. And that's what it is: writing about my experiences and about the issue of masturbation in general. I would love readers who like masturbation as much as I do to add their own contribution to the Journal. So please join . . .

16 July 2007
Years ago I conceived the plan of starting a journal in which I would record my masturbatory activities. I never got round to it, although I occasionally wrote about in my ordinary diary. The fact that I'm finally starting on it after all those years is not without reason.

Masturbation is not an easy subject to talk about. I'm no exception to the rule. However frequently and however pleasurably I masturbate, until recently talking about it has always been taboo, except in the shady world of sex chatrooms. But even there masturbation is almost always treated as a second-rate form of sex, 'for want of anything better'.

It was only very recently that I discovered a website on the net linked to a Yahoo group, entirely devoted to men who see masturbation as the ultimate form of sex and use it frequently in their lives. It opened up a whole new world to me. I wasn't the only one and I wasn't an exception. That discovery gave me a hug feeling of liberation, even stronger than when I came out of the closet as a gay man.

Via the Yahoo group I came into contact with a Dutch masturbator and later by a different internet route two chronic onanists. And so I entered that fascinating kingdom called Onania, ruled by the god of fertility and the male sex organ, Priapus.

My original plan was to keep this diary in the form of a weblog, but the snag with blogs is that people can usually respond immediately and so I would constantly have to remove undesirable responses and block readers. That doesn't appeal to me. I'd rather spend the time on a long masturbation session. But I did want to put the journal online, freely available to all. That's why people can respond by email. Apart from that, I'm not going to advertise the journal and will only give the link to enthusiastic fellow-masturbators. I'm convinced that it will soon start to become accessible via search engines, since which of us has never entered 'masturbation' as a search term?

I have resolved not to let the personal nature of this journal be an obstacle to my writing freely about and describing my masturbation experiences. In order to preserve the journal character I have decided against a fancy website design. That doesn't mean of course that I shan't occasionally add visuals. Enough introducing, commenting and explaining, I think. Time to get down to the real (manual) work.

17 July

Yesterday I had a long masturbation session, partly by email in contact with V. a chronic fellow-masturbator I met through the Onania Support Group. After he dropped out I went on jerking off for another half-hour, always trying to master and refine the art of 'edging'. This morning at ten o'clock I was back masturbating at my laptop, legs wide apart with a huge morning erection, in anticipation of a message from V. about a possible joint telephone session. He made contact after about an hour, but by then I had no time left. Again I had no ejaculation and no orgasm.

I got into the car for my fortnightly drive from U. to S., about two hundred kilometres. With my jeans pulled down slightly I started masturbating as soon as I got to the motorway. I had done it often before, but never with such intensity, so aware of the horniness and arousal in every fibre of my body. I reached a kind of ecstatic state, without losing concentration on the road. My surroundings, though, faded completely into the background, and I felt the journey had had never been so quick. Even more than the fact that I hadn't come for two days, I attribute this to the newly acquired freedom I've experienced since discovering the Brotherhood of Onanists, as I'll call the network for now.

It took a little getting used to after nineteen days, the exact period during which my masturbation adventures really took off. Different house, difference sounds, different laptop, different place to sit. Apart from that a dog and a cat around the whole time, though I know from experience that they haven't the slightest interest in my sexual escapades.

V. made no further contact that evening and the thirty-something with whom I had chatted to the previous evening on MSN about our chronic urge to masturbate also failed to show up. No panic, there's always x-tube. The gay section is full of clips of masturbating, jerking and wanking men, who seem to want nothing better than to demonstrate their skills to the world. It seems almost a dereliction of duty if you have not yet joined the ranks of x-tube. I put three men with various clips into my Favourites folder, precisely because their clips show them to be masters of edging, not forgetting the verbal expression of their ecstasy: grunting, groaning, talking dirty, completely absorbed in their excitement, proud of the hardness and fullness of their sex. Apart from that all three of them are uncircumcised and all my life I've simply had a thing about foreskins, so that's an extra bonus.

Getting aroused and having an erection was not a problem, but I could no longer manage edging, let alone coming. The moralist in me reared his head for a moment: you've been overdoing it recently of course. I know better than that. The new onanism has only strengthened my sex drive, my erections are stronger and more powerful than they have been for a long time and my ejaculations too are growing stronger every day. To say nothing of those wonderful, explosive orgasms after a lengthy session. No, I was simply too tired after eight days' work combined with a Dutch gin on the rocks. And luckily I can allow myself to feel tired. Tomorrow is another day, the second of five days off.

18 July

Sex with the same person has never kept its charm for me for very long, not even in two long-term relationships. That's why I always paid for sex outside, quite openly, though. But whether in or out of the relationship, the urge to masturbate always remained strong and I always gave in to it. One of the long-term relationships ran aground because of lack of sex. I knew at once that it was my fault, without being able to explain the exact reason, because the sex we had was not at all bad. And the sex I had elsewhere was often hopeless, or at least I didn't find what I was looking for in it. Only now, years later and having come into contact with the Worldwide Brotherhood of Onanists, am I beginning to understand and has the penny dropped: for me the best sex there is, is sex with myself. And that has always been the case. It's just that I've never seen it like that, approached it like that, let alone said it aloud to myself, as I do now. I've always given in to the urge to masturbate. I've never felt guilty about it. In general any kind of moralising about sex is alien to me. The idea that masturbation might be my main sexual preference never occurred to me. But that has now changed forever and I intend to make the most of it.

Nearly one in the morning. At ten last night started on a long masturbation session. Earlier in the day V. emailed me to say he was planning to have a digital masturbation session until midnight. But, doubtless for good reasons, he did not make contact. After an hour of jerking off, edging, stopping and continuing I was completely high. But this time the high went further, deeper. The whole room, already shrouded in darkness because I had only one lamp lit next to me on the table, fell away completely. I was alone with my body and the laptop, with my favourite x-tube clips, which I replayed again and again. It was as if every fibre of my being was flooding with pure horniness. The moment I felt the climax approaching and stopped, the inside of my thighs began to tingle, my penis made violent jerking movements, and the ecstasy of the moment flowed through my abdomen. In the hour that followed those sensations went on growing and I felt as if my prick was growing longer, harder and thicker than ever before and was going a darker colour than I had ever experienced. Even without a cock ring the veins directly below the skin swelled up and I said to myself: this is the height of maleness, of proud virility.

20 July

An interesting and exciting evening, yesterday. First a long chat on MSN with G., mainly about our own experiences, motives and feelings during and about masturbation. G. draws on a rich arsenal of experiences and is a keen raconteur. His predilection is mainly masturbating with others, seeing and being seen.

The chat branched out into all aspects of the noble art and at a certain moment I let slip the word 'addiction'. Am I addicted, and if so, what do I think about it? I said I thought it was a nice addiction. G. asked about possible negative sides and that set me thinking. I know a lot about addictions because of my work, and so I can easily imagine all sorts of things when it comes to those less positive aspects. I encounter signs in Yahoo groups. There are men who avoid social contacts or sometimes no longer have any social interaction at all, men who regularly take time off work on medical grounds or on some other pretext to have more time and opportunity to masturbate. I can imagine what they feel like to some extent, but in my case it's a matter of trying to use the time and opportunities that present themselves to the full.

G. and I chatted for nearly an hour and a half. I got tired and wanted to conserve some energy for my night-time session. Before I turned the laptop off I decided to check my mail. I found that V. had been in touch and from that moment on the horny emails flew back and forth, as we masturbated and turned each other on in the most explicit terms. Only with him do I have that fraternal feeling, and especially when he started calling me brother and later little brother. I like being a little brother and seeing him as a big brother, more experienced and practised in chronic masturbation and edging. We didn't come on this occasion, but we didn't mind. It was a mutual affirmation and we both look forward to having a horny jerk-off session in the flesh.

This morning before I got up J. and I had sex. I went down on him and he gave me a hand job. Although I produced a lot of sperm, I didn't have a really powerful orgasm, so it dribbled down my still erect cock towards my balls. He knows that I jerk off regularly, but he doesn't know much about the details and he's ignorant of recent developments. At the moment I still have no desire at all to share it with him. Maybe I will later.

21 July
Yesterday evening at about ten I started on my masturbation session. Halfway through and after several near-climaxes I suddenly realized that my erection was a lot harder that during sex with J. that morning. That must say something. When I couldn't find anyone online at eleven o'clock, I stopped and went to bed without having come but with an intense horny feeling right through my body. During the night I must have woken up at least four times with a huge hard-on, which because I was so sleepy I did nothing about. I suspect I had wild dreams, but I can't remember a thing about them.

This morning two emails from my brother in masturbation V. He had been online looking for a horny digital jerk-off session, but I was already asleep at the time. That's how it goes when you're not alone and have got a social life, which applies both to him and to me – a drag sometimes.

The two-hundred-kilometre drive from S. to U. in the early afternoon. Twice spent half an hour jerking off at the wheel, four or so times up to the border, horny and already looking forward to the next chance to masturbate.

7

Culture, Religions and Philosophers

'Go forth and multiply,' as it says in Genesis. Down the ages, generally speaking, spilling one's seed has been regarded as sinful or as a necessary evil in most cultures and religions. The history of the safeguarding of the position of sexual intercourse for the purpose of reproduction is an immensely long one. In fact it begins from a religious point of view with Genesis and culturally in the fourth century BC with Plato (427–347) in his *Symposium*, where he describes a banquet at which all the guests sing the praises of love. The playwright Aristophanes (448–380 BC), who was present, is reported to have presented a view of human nature that had three forms: the male, the female and a hybrid of the two called 'androgynous' in a positive sense. These androgynes planned an attack on the gods, to which the gods responded by cleaving the representatives of the third sex in two! Since then, so the story goes, human beings have been searching for complete reunion in the form of the sexual act, implicitly labelling masturbation as an inferior activity.

The granddaddy of masturbation anxiety and especially of fear of tuberculosis of the spine was the Greek doctor and philosopher Hippocrates (460–375 BC). He was concerned not only with the condemning practice of masturbation but especially with the weakening of the human body through ejaculation. Galen (AD 131–199), of Greek origin and personal physician to the emperor Marcus Aurelius, held quite opposite views: sexual intercourse and masturbation served to keep the body healthy and to protect it against harmful toxins. He believed that sexual abstinence could cause tremors, fits and madness. Those wishing to study Galen's writings can find them in the *Loeb Classical Library Series.* Like Galen, the Muslim philosopher and doctor Avicenna (980–1037) expressed a positive view on the habit among doctors of recommending it where sexual intercourse was not possible.

Mythology

To my knowledge there is only one culture in which masturbation plays a part in the story of creation, namely the Ancient Egyptian. The Egyptians believed that life arose from the dark and amorphous emptiness of Nun, the waters of chaos. At the beginning of time a mountain of earth rose up from Nun, an event that subsequently took place figuratively each year when the land re-emerged after the water of the flooding Nile had subsided. It was upon that mountain that the gods created life.

Each of the principal temples of Heliopolis, Hermopolis and Memphis laid a claim to be the site of the primeval mountain. In Heliopolis the sun god Atum was regarded as the principal creator. He appeared at the first sunrise from the lotus flower, a flower that sprouted from the primeval mountain. According to tradition Atum carried the life force of the universe in himself. With that force he created the twin deities Shu, the god of light, and Tefnut, goddess of wetness. Atum did this either by masturbating with his

Atum Masturbates with his Mouth, Egyptian papyrus.

hand or by ejaculating or, as another, bowdlerized version of the myth has it, by 'sneezing out Shu and spewing out Tefnut'. The latter description at any rate alludes to a version in which Atum performs fellatio on himself.

The Greek God Hermes is supposed to have taught his son Pan to masturbate after the latter had been repeatedly rejected by nymphs, among them Echo. Is it true? The question of who Pan's parents were is a little confusing. Sometimes he is called the son of Hermes and Penelope (Odysseus' wife), sometimes the son of Zeus and the nymph Callisto, or else the son of Hermes and Amalthea. Pan was depicted with cloven hooves, with the body and head of a man and with horns. He was the symbol of fertility, and was lewd and horny. Pan was always chasing nymphs and constantly falling in love. Unfortunately they always fled, as they found him dreadfully ugly.

One day Pan was pursuing a very chaste nymph called Syrinx. Just as he was about to grab hold of her, one of her sisters turned her into a reed stalk (the events took place on the banks of the River Ladon. Since Pan did not know what reed stalk she was hiding in, he cut off a number of stalks and made them into a flute. Thus the Pan pipes became his trademark. The instrument con-

Pan, the oversexed woodland god.

sists of seven pipes of decreasing length. Pan was able to draw the most mellifluous and seductive melodies from his pipes, but when he was in a bad mood you could hear his roaring for miles, which is why the word panic is derived from this woodland god who at the same time is the first Greek masturbator. Panic strikes suddenly, widely and is usually unfounded.

The physical depiction of Pan and other demigods or woodland deities was adopted by Christianity to represent the devil. Pan himself, so the story goes, was condemned for centuries to teach lonely shepherds how to masturbate.

The Greek philosopher Diogenes considered masturbation superior to all other forms of gratification, and indulged in it quite happily, as is clear from a poem by Agathias (536–580) in the *Greek Anthology*:

By what road shall one go to the Land of Love? If you seek him in the streets, you will repent of the courtesan's greed for gold and luxury. If you approach a maiden's bed, it must end in lawful wedlock or punishment for seduction. Who would endure to awake reluctant desire for his lawful wife, forced to do a duty? Adulterous intercourse is the worst of all and has no part in love, and unnatural sin should be ranked with it. As for widows, if one is ill-conducted, she is anyone's mistress, and knows all the arts of harlotry, while if she is chaste she with difficulty consents, she is pricked by loveless remorse, hates what she has done, and having a remnant of shame shrinks from the union till she is disposed to announce its end. If you associate with your own servant, you must make up your mind to change places and become hers, and if with someone else's, the law which prosecutes for outrage on slaves not one's own will mark you with infamy. *All of these perils Diogenes escaped by singing his nuptial song with his hand, having no need for a beautiful partner.*

A classicist pointed out to me that the penultimate line could be translated differently, namely: Diogenes escaped, he was in the habit of singing the wedding song to his hand. He had no need for Lais! Lais was a woman of loose morals from Corinth, who was famed for her exceptional beauty, as shown by the fact that Agathias was still talking about her at the time of Justinian.

Back to Diogenes. In fact, his reasoning was as follows: if eating is the most natural thing in the world, then you should have no qualms about doing it in public. Eating *is* the most natural thing in the world, so there is nothing wrong in doing it in public. So logically he also masturbated in public, saying, 'Oh, if only I could drive hunger away by rubbing my belly like that!'

The Old Testament and Judaism

It is important to make a distinction between masturbation and onanism. For those not brought up with the Scriptures, the term onanism is quite wrongly derived from Onan, a grandson of the patriarch Jacob. According to ancient Jewish custom, Onan's father demanded that he marry Tamar, the widow of his dead brother and beget children with her. Onan was unwilling and 'it came to pass, when he went in unto his brother's wife, that he spilled it [his seed] on the ground, lest that he should give seed to his brother' (Genesis 38: 1–30).

The name of Judah's second son Onan means something like 'powerful'. So Onan has it in him, but does nothing with it, and has quite wrongly given his name to masturbation or onanism. Dictionaries define the term as meaning either masturbation or coitus interruptus. The Christian tradition has always linked the two activities with Onan's spilling of his seed on the ground and condemned it roundly. One can find the same sentiment in the visual arts, for example in a rather weird drawing by the obscure German draughtsman and illustrator Otto Hundt (b. 1887). The

Otto Hundt,
The Unborn Pursue the Sinner, early 20th-century pen-and-ink drawing.

theme is also found in poetry, for example in H. P. Bosman's poem 'Patriarch':

> In every drop of seed that I misplace
> Cell by cell my progeny are lost.
> Alone, I pay rash calculation's cost.
> Unnumbered is the death I cannot face.

And in 'Saldo mortis':

> Today, once more, Death writes to punish me:
> 'Yet again you haven't tried to live,
> you're overdrawn. What have you got to give?'
> I jot a poem, and wank obediently.

In old manuals coitus was rather bizarrely called 'marital onanism'. In the Jewish tradition masturbation has been traditionally severely condemned. The Talmud makes no bones about it: unmarried men are forbidden to hold their penises even while urinating. For that reason among orthodox Jews one of the main aspects of hygiene training is that a boy is constantly being warned against touching his penis. 'No hands,' is the warning cry. Better to aim badly than to learn a bad habit! All this is connected with the fact that in Jewish law spontaneous ejaculations are seen partly as sinful. The ancient legislators were convinced that touching the penis during the day could lead to more nocturnal emissions. Married men, though, are allowed to take hold of the penis to guide it into the vagina.

To make it absolutely clear: the Jewish ban on masturbation is not directed against sexual pleasure. The Judaic tradition has always been more broad-minded in this respect than the Christian: of course one is allowed to enjoy sex, since it is a fundamental human need. No, the prohibition on masturbation is directed mainly against spilling one's seed, seed with its potential for creating human life. It is no accident that in rabbinical Hebrew a 'descendant' was often called 'seed'.

The anti-psychiatrist Thomas Szasz (1920–) argued that Judaism's ban on touching the penis symbolizes the idea that the man's sex organs belong to the Jewish god. Theologically speaking the Jewish requirement of circumcision symbolizes the union between Jahweh and Abraham. In Szasz's view the two customs are linked: only a circumcised man can urinate without touching his penis, as an uncircumcised man has to slide back his foreskin. The ritual of circumcision is required in order to make the ban on touching the penis possible.

If one is to believe the Talmud, women have more sexual options. The rabbi, scholar, doctor and philosopher Maimonides (1135–1204) writes that a woman may obtain sexual gratification without having a man approach her. So masturbation is allowed for women, no seed is spilled and sexual pleasure is in no way forbidden. The ban is consequently directed at men, and the main issue is the destination of the seed.

Onan

Therefore, as Eewout van der Linden argues in his book *Adam and Eve's Apple*, the story of Onan and Tamar is not about masturbation, but about coitus interruptus. Ejaculation outside the vagina is meant to prevent Tamar from becoming pregnant, since her firstborn son would not continue Onan's line but that of his dead brother Er. It is not so much coitus interruptus that is the problem as the refusal to do one's brotherly duty by spilling potentially life-giving seed. Onan sabotages his duty as a brother-in-law towards Tamar. His intention is to prevent his brother's name from being continued.

But what does the duty of a brother-in-law actually consist of? In his above-mentioned book Van der Linden explains that in the story of Tamar the duty of a brother-in-law is presented in a stricter light than in the passage from Deuteronomy (25:5-10). What does it come down to? When two brothers live together and one of them dies without having produced a son, the wife of the dead man is not allowed to marry outside the family. Her brother-in-law will have intercourse with her, take her as his wife and in so doing conclude a 'brother-in-law's marriage', also called a leviratical marriage (*levir* means brother-in-law). If a son is born, he must be treated as the son of the dead brother. The purpose of leviratical marriage was to preserve the name of the dead man. Without a patriarch your line dies out. This is based on more than just emotion; it also involves the law of succession and the loss of family property in the case of childlessness. In other words, sex in the service of economics.

There were, however, ways of escaping leviratical marriage. If the couple could really not stand each other, the brother-in-law could refuse. The daughter-in-law then had to go to 'the elders of the city in the gate' and explain the case, after which the brother-in-law had to publicly renounce his right. The accompanying ritual was for the sister-in-law to take off her brother-in-law's shoe, spit in his face and publicly denounce him as someone who was failing in his duty. To make a long story short: Onan could therefore have avoided his duty, since the law gave him the opportunity. The legal statutes did not, however, provide for the eventuality of the sister-in-law wanting nothing to do with her brother-in-law.

Ezekiel

The Old Testament book of the prophet Ezekiel contains chapters that are notoriously sexually explicit. The sexual terminology is extremely direct, especially in those chapters that mercilessly ridicule the political and religious apostasy of Israel and Judea, the Northern Kingdom and the Southern Kingdom.

In Chapter 16 there is a passing reference to masturbation. The priest Ezekiel worked in Babylonia in the years 593–571 BC. In various waves of deportation the upper echelons of Jewish society had been taken into exile in Babylon by King Nebuchadnezzar who had destroyed Jerusalem in 586. The Northern Kingdom of Israel had fallen long before, in 721 BC. The theme of the prophet is the downfall and restoration of Israel and Judea. In two infamous chapters, 16 and 23, he compares the two kingdoms to two sisters who have thrown away their marriage with God. The prophet looks back at the history of the nations since their period in Egypt down to their exile and can only conclude that its whole course was chaotic. The language is so full of sexual allusions that later translations and adaptations of this chapter were bowdlerized. The words of Ezekiel are put into the mouth of God Himself: He is the male accuser, the deceived spouse, the furious husband.

In the first instance Chapter 16 describes in moving and tender images how vulnerable Jerusalem originally was. The city is compared to a newborn child that has no one to cut its umbilical cord. The baby was casually abandoned in a ploughed field, and no one paid it any attention. Then God sees it, and the prophet gives a penetrating description of how God takes the child under his wing, brings it up and marries it:

> And when I passed by thee, and saw thee polluted in thine own blood, I said unto thee when thou wast in thy blood, Live; yea, I said unto thee when thou wast in thy blood, Live.
>
> I have caused thee to multiply as the bud of the field, and thou hast increased and waxen great, and thou art come to excellent ornaments; thy breasts are fashioned, and thine hair is grown, whereas thou was naked and bare.
>
> Now when I passed by thee, and looked upon thee, behold thy time was the time of love; and I spread my skirt over thee, and covered thy nakedness: yea, I sware unto thee, and entered into a covenant with thee, saith the Lord God, and thou becamest mine. (Ezekiel 16:6–8)

God anoints her with oil, and gives her the finest clothes and jewellery. Her beauty is perfection, but then her troubles begin: having become reckless with her beauty and fame, she throws away all she has. 'But thou didst trust in thine own beauty, and playedst the harlot because of thy renown, and pourest out thy fornications on every one that passed by; his it was. And of thy garments thou didst take, and deckedst thy high places with divers colours, and playedst the harlot thereupon' (Ezekiel 16:15–16). She even made male images from her jewels, with which she masturbated (this is the only possible interpretation).

For God she has overstepped the mark. He begins to reproach his adulterous wife. How could she forget her childhood? How could she throw herself away like that? 'Thou hast opened thy feet to every one that passed by . . .' God accuses her: 'Thou hast also committed fornication with the Egyptians thy neighbours, great of flesh.' In the New English Bible, the King James Bible's 'great of flesh' has become 'sexually aroused'. Whichever way you look at it, the language is fairly steamy.

God is furious at her sexual behaviour and lashes out at her:

> Because thy filthiness was poured out, and thy nakedness dis-
> covered through thy whoredoms with thy lovers, and with all
> the idols of thy abominations ... therefore will I gather all thy
> lovers, with whom thou hast taken pleasure, with all them that
> thou hast hated; I will even gather them round about against
> thee, and will discover thy nakedness unto them, that they
> may see all thy nakedness. And I will judge thee, as women
> that break wedlock and shed blood are judged; and I will give
> thee blood in fury and jealousy (Ezekiel 16:36–38)

Her lovers will pull off her clothes, and unleash a mob on her who
will stone her and hack at her with swords. Only then will God
become calmer and cease to be angry.

In a kind of postscript God compares the behaviour of Jerusalem in the Southern Kingdom to that of her equally adulterous
sisters in the Northern Kingdom, Sodom and Gomorrah. The
sisters are three of a kind, though Jerusalem's behaviour has been
more outrageous. Compared with Jerusalem Sodom and Gomorrah seem righteous. But after their humiliation God will improve
their lot, and will again make a pact with them.

Ezekiel's intention is clear. He wants to show quite unambiguously that God has had enough. From exile he offers a retrospec-
tive view of past history: in the eyes of the prophet this often
represents the complete surrender of Israel and Judea to the great
powers of Egypt and Babylonia, their gods and their abominable
practices.

So much for the Bible.

The Christian Churches

The Catholic Church believes that masturbation is a morally
disordered act because the deliberate use of one's sexual powers

outside normal marital relations is in conflict with the finality of those relations. The masturbator seeks gratification outside a sexual relationship, outside a relationship that embodies the full meaning of mutual giving and human procreation in the context of true love. Paragraph 2352 of the *Catechism of the Catholic Church* (1997) says in so many words that masturbation ('the deliberate stimulation of the genital organs in order to derive sexual pleasure') is a morally disordered act. It involves something that is contrary to the producing of children.

In order to reach a fair assessment of the moral responsibility of those involved and to give guidance for pastoral care, the Catholic Church does, however, maintain that account must be taken of immature feelings, the power of habit, anxiety or social factors. All of these can lessen the 'moral' guilt, or even reduce it to a minimum.

All the Catholic agonizing about masturbation began long before 1995, but at the beginning everything in the garden appeared to be lovely. I am referring to the period in which the later Pope John XXI (1215–1277) wrote his works. Portuguese by birth, before his election he lived under the name of Peter of Spain. After studying theology in Paris he was appointed Professor of Medicine at the University of Siena, and there wrote *Quaestiones super Viaticum*, in which he wondered who experienced the most pleasure in sex, the man or the woman. His answer was: the man in terms of 'quality' and the woman in terms of 'quantity'. Seven hundred years later Masters and Johnson were to support his assertion: orgasms usually last longer in women than in men, and women are capable of climaxing several times in succession. In *Thesaurus Paperum*, the mostly widely read medical book in the thirteenth century, John XXI presented 56 recipes for strengthening male potency. Sadly he was killed after he had been pope for nine months when the ceiling of his library suddenly collapsed. A misfortune for Western civilization! Or a timely signal from on high? His successors at any rate had different ideas about sex.

Coitus was regarded as a 'brain drain' and sperm was an abomination. Endless discussions were conducted on such questions as whether demons also produced sperm. The Vatican believed that evil spirits sprang from sexual contact between fallen angels and women. But that still left the question where the demons got their sperm from. Did it mean the last emission from hanged criminals? Or sperm deriving from masturbators? Or from people who practised coitus interruptus? The scholars could not decide, but Thomas Aquinas (1225–1274) finally did. In *Quaestiones Quodlibetales* and *Summa Theologica* he explained that demons assumed the form of a woman ('succubus') in order to seduce a man. Afterwards the demons would assume the form of a man and use the previously obtained seed to impregnate the unsuspecting woman secretly. He regarded masturbation as a crime, which in his view was worse than having sexual intercourse with one's own mother.

In the later Middle Ages the Church issued a long list of prohibitions which contained descriptions of every sin which had its own accompanying penance. Masturbation scored high on the list. The severity of the penalty depended on a person's age and marital and religious status.

When Canon Johann von Wesel was tried before a heretics' court in Mainz in 1479 (*Eunuchs for the Kingdom of Heaven*, 1991) orality was the only issue. Medical counter-arguments carried no weight with the court. The point was that the canon had acquainted himself with the theories of Galen and Avicenna and fully embraced them. In his writings Von Wesel dealt with the question of whether monks could fall ill as a result of abstinence. He wondered whether it was permissible to remove sperm that had gone bad and was poisoning the body in some artificial way, though without causing pleasurable sensations. He even questioned whether a possible sensation of pleasure might not be free of sin, especially if the cleansing process was purely in the interests of health. Johan von Wesel's apotheosis was forced recantation of his writings and a sentence of lifelong incarceration in a monastery.

The seventeenth-century masturbation delusion, largely inspired by the Calvinist physician Tissot, was grist to the mill of Catholic moral theology. Diabolical punishments in the hereafter might not be exactly a treat, but for most people the prospect of a dreadful disease in their earthly life was much more alarming. This gave the theologians, as proclaimers of God's will, both proof and legitimacy. And so the Church began using the medical misconceptions in all sorts of writings and treatises large and small, especially those intended for young people. The same applied for that matter to the fledgling Protestant Churches. In 1640 Richard Capel, chaplain of Magdalen College, Oxford, argued in his book *Temptations, their Nature, their Peril, their Cure* that self-abuse was the greatest sin against nature and brought with it physical weakness, impotence in marriage, shortening of one's lifespan and suicide. At this period Magdalen College was *the* centre of Protestant Puritanism.

In 1842 the influential moral theologian, Trappist and doctor Father J. C. Debreyne published a controversial article on the consequences of masturbation. It was the familiar litany of woes, though he did have very original recommendations for those afflicted with masturbation: they should sleep only on their side, never on their backs, stick to cold food and drink, suck on ice cubes, take cold showers with meltwater mixed with kitchen salt, etc. One detail that is worth mentioning is that this Dutch monk argued for removal of the clitoris, 'since it was not necessary for procreation'.

In the 1930s Leslie Weatherhead's *The Mastery of Sex through Psychology and Religion* became a bestseller. One of his main contentions was that for thousands of English men and women masturbation was the greatest problem in their life and provoked 'neuroses'. He warned against seeing masturbation as something positive; it was a sin and the Christian religion offered the way out. As late as 1947 a man was excommunicated for refusing treatment for his 'onanistic neurosis'.

In 1967 Bernhard Häring wrote in the eighth edition of the moral-theological work *Das Gesetz Christi* that masturbation has harmful consequences for health. He did, though, admit that harm to health might not be experienced if the masturbation were not excessive and so offered a shred of hope to intimidated Catholics. And this was in the liberated 1960s!

Once again a pope became involved. In 1975 Pope Paul VI condemned the 'grievous sin' of masturbation in a statement on some sexual and ethical problems. After doctors and pedagogues had slowly distanced themselves from masturbation, it was threatening to fall into the hands of theologians once again. Those who masturbate 'lose God's love', wrote God's representative on earth. And a little further on: 'Masturbation is a grievous sin, although it is impossible to demonstrate unambiguously that the Holy Scriptures expressly reject sin as such.'

In 1985 the Church of Rome received help from the east, from of all places a country that instead of an ecclesiastical ban on contraceptives operated state-imposed compulsory contraception. Uta Ranke-Heinemann describes this in her book *Eunuchs for the Kingdom of Heaven*. The episode centred on a study trip by a number of German moral theologians in collaboration with the German conference of bishops, whose intention was to build bridges with the isolated Catholic Church in China.

One of the participants wrote: 'In order to implement the birth control programme intensive educational campaigns were organized. Young people were encouraged to observe sexual abstinence. They were guided (in 1985) by the following pronouncements: 1. early marriage is harmful and leads to excessive sexuality 2. an intensive sex life leads to impotence 3. masturbation results in impotence, brain damage and short-sightedness 4. the following counter-measures are recommended: a. study of the works of Marx, Lenin and Mao b. gymnastics c. early rising d. the avoidance of sleeping on one's abdomen e. the avoidance of hot blankets f. avoidance of close-fitting underwear and g. plenty of shadow boxing.'

Back in 1985 China with its one-child families was clearly a promising field for its gospel of abstinence. And it was to their advantage that the Chinese became short-sighted and promised even greater attention to the good tidings of the Church of Rome!

One last anecdote about a pope, that is, John Paul II: in 1990 the celebrated pop singer Madonna began her second world tour, the Blonde Ambition Tour, a perfectly orchestrated, tightly organized show, marked by a lot of swearing and sexual gestures. What caused particular controversy was the infamous performance of the Oriental version of the song *Like a Virgin*. During the number Madonna kept feeling her covered breasts, grabbed her crotch and at the climax she masturbated and simulated an orgasm by thrashing about on her back on a bed while being groped by two of the chorus of dancers. The show was regarded as controversial because of the use of Roman Catholic symbols such as the cross and priest's and nun's habits. Pope John Paul II appealed to Catholics to boycott the show, and Madonna had to cancel one performance in Rome. She was furious and invited the pope to attend one of her shows, but he did not accept her invitation.

Islam

The opinions of Muslim theologians on masturbation differ widely. Neither contemporary nor earlier Islamic scholars forbid masturbation under all circumstances. In order to avoid adultery or vice (*zina*) *al-istimma bi'l-ya*, masturbation is permitted, although it remains a practice that is disapproved of, says Abdulhawid van Bommel, a leading Dutch Muslim. However, masturbation is not regarded as *zina*, even if a man is masturbated by a woman who is not his wife. In the past some scholars were even more sceptical about one's own hand than that of a female slave. Yet if a case became publicly known it could lead to a disciplinary punishment, especially if it happened purely out of lust.

In all Koranic schools masturbation is permitted in the case of long-term isolation or if there is a risk of homosexual relationships, for instance in prison. Nothing is ever said about this in Christian circles. Some Hanbali scholars permitted women to use the 'kirandi', a dildo made from animal skin, when their husband was away for an extended period. Again, I have never heard a Protestant vicar tackle this issue.

Like the Church Fathers, Muslim scholars direct their criticisms of masturbation mainly at the important part that fantasy usually plays in it. Fantasizing about other partners could open the way to adultery and homosexual relationships. The most nuanced views are found in the school of Abu Hanifa. The Hanafi school (one of the four schools of Sunni Muslims) was the earliest established under the jurist Imam Abu Hanifa, who was born and taught in Iraq. His school differed from the other three in many areas, including the type of punishments meted out for various crimes in Islam.

Taoism

It is not only the three Semitic religions that have a negative view of auto-eroticism. In Taoism masturbation is seen as pure sex – without warmth, without feeling, communication or harmony of *yin* and *yang*. Masturbation by the man means the loss of vital yang juices without the compensation of acquiring vital yin liquid in return. The act is futile.

In his book *The Tao of Love and Sex* Jolan Chang writes that he is probably one of the few men who have not masturbated more than a dozen times in their life. 'I felt that masturbation was a mechanical process and that there was no poetry in it.' He places the emphasis on control of the ejaculation, not only in masturbation but also in coitus. The Tao masters regard male sperm as a very important life-giving liquid. 'If a man spills his seed he will fall ill and if he exhausts his seed thoughtlessly he will die.'

The concern about loss of sperm is still topical in Asia. Indian doctors see a large number of male patients who are diagnosed with the 'Dhat syndrome'. The manifestations are loss of sperm and all kinds of weaknesses and anxieties. It is difficult for the Western observer to establish whether these patients simply have a hypochondriacal attitude to masturbation, such as our fore-fathers had, or whether there really is a kind of physiological state in which the man 'leaks' sperm. According to modern views a man does start to leak sperm after fourteen days' abstinence, but this takes place via the urine.

Not that long ago the spilling of seed was equated with the loss of mental energy in Europe too. Thanks to the journals of the De Goncourt brothers we know that Flaubert, on his regular visits to prostitutes, always tried to use *coitus reservatus*, that is, to avoid ejaculation. 'Hier, j'ai perdu un livre' (Yesterday, I lost a book), he confided sadly to the brothers, indicating obliquely that his sperm had once again escaped him.

The Taoist stress a tender and sensitive approach to love and sex. At the same time they point to the importance of acquired skills. If you want to play the piano, you start with five-finger exercises and if you want to paint you first need to know some-thing about composition and draughtsmanship. In a similar way men and women must learn how to love each other. The French novelist Honoré de Balzac (1799–1850) said long ago that a clumsy lover is comparable to an ape trying to play the violin. He was right: a clumsy lover can give a woman the impression that he is masturbating in her vagina. The writer Germaine Greer (1939–) described such an experience in *The Female Eunuch*:

When a man is ashamed to masturbate, and instead waylays women for the sake of finding sexual release, the shame that should attach to the masturbatory activity, not significantly different in such a case except that the friction was provided by a female organ and the ejaculation may occur in the vagina, is referred to the woman.

The Tao dictates that the man develop his skill in love, so that he can both appreciate and satisfy his partner. That means not so much the provision of immediate pleasure, but embraces at a deeper, more metaphysical level the promotion of mutual contentment.

Modern philosophers

Immanuel Kant (1724–1804), a German philosopher of the Enlightenment, is regarded as the first German idealist. He was the fourth of nine children of a poor saddler. At the age of eight, through the good offices of a Pietist clergyman, Kant was able to attend the Collegium Fridericianum, a Latin school in his home town of Königsberg. When he was sixteen he went to university, where he studied first theology and afterwards philosophy, mathematics and physics. In 1770 Kant became professor of metaphysics and logic in the faculty of philosophy at the University of Königsberg. His influence is still felt today in the fields of philosophy, ethics, theology, criminal law, international law and aesthetics. He also expressed a view on masturbation, in an odd way, at least for a 'man of the Enlightenment'. He was violently opposed to it and considered it a completely unnatural phenomenon. Sex should be focused on reproduction and was intended first and foremost for the maintenance of the species, which in his eyes made masturbation worse than suicide. Kant saw it as a bestial trait and the masturbator as lacking in any kind of self-respect. 'A person loses his personality' and 'deprives himself of any kind of self-respect' if he uses his body 'simply as a means to satisfy an animal urge'. In the *Treatise on Pedagogy* (1786) he writes that by masturbating one exhausts one's strength and can expect an early death. In order to resist temptation Kant's advice was to be sure to keep fully occupied and not to spend more time sleeping than was strictly necessary. In that way one could steer clear of evil.

Another German philosopher, Arthur Schopenhauer (1788–1860), had a decidedly pessimistic world view. In 1805 his father was fatally injured in a fall in a warehouse. His mother, Johanna, moved in circles close to Goethe and the young Schopenhauer seemed to be looking for a substitute father figure in him, but a rift soon developed between the two self-confident thinkers.

In Schopenhauer's view in *The World as Will and Representation* (1818) masturbation is 'more reprehensible' than sexual intercourse. The latter is the strongest possible affirmation of life, and its motive is the wish to view life in its 'complete' revelation: the human form. Masturbation is an affirmation of the body only; hence life is not affirmed, only the body. In this way, says Schopenhauer, man is acting like a plant. One could counter by saying that in many cases, certainly in the twenty-first century, sexual intercourse has degenerated into a simple affirmation of bodies. The Idea, as he calls it, has no part in it. In many cases of auto-eroticism the Idea is definitely a part. It is an idealized desire, idealized fantasies and an idealized anticipation of the result.

Schopenhauer may be right when he wants to establish a dividing line, but that line divides two forms of masturbation, between those people who live according to the material and those who live according to the spiritual. Someone who, like Schopenhauer, reproaches sensual love with having dragged him down from heavenly heights and cast him into the dust bound hand and foot, is not the best guide to lead us towards the Idea, since he or she has trodden the path in the opposite direction.

Friedrich Nietzsche (1844–1900) began writing autobiographical sketches from the age of twelve and at the end of his life produced the magnificent self-dramatization *Ecce Homo*. Nietzsche's first commandment was to be master and shaper of himself. He saw himself as both director and actor in a play of his own making. In his study of Nietzsche, Peter Claessens reviews

the principal 'primal scenes' in the life of the philosopher and
composer, dramatic moments that were decisive for the development of his thought. In a whirl of enthusiasm the author follows
Nietzsche through all his metamorphoses. After his break with
Richard Wagner (1883), the artist with whom he felt most affinity,
Nietzsche is mortified when he hears that the same Wagner, in a
correspondence with his doctors in about 1876, has explained
the sudden change in his thinking as the result of excessive
masturbation.

Georges Bataille (1897–1962) was the child of a mentally
unstable mother and father who suffered from syphilis. The
horrors of the First World War made a profound impression on
him. Having been brought up as a Catholic he at first sought sanctuary in faith, but in his twenties he turned away from the Church.
At that time he began a spiritual quest that was to occupy him for
the rest of his life and took him via the philosophy of Nietzsche
and Marx to Sigmund Freud. Bataille tried to understand human
behaviour on the basis of psychology, especially incongruous, un-
couth and scandalous behaviour, including masturbation. Bataille
took from Freud the notion that man is essentially driven by two
paradoxically opposed urges: the life urge and the death urge. The
life urge is the easiest of the two to understand: no one wants to
die. We try to achieve what we have not been able to accomplish
as an individual – eternal life – for our species. Hence our
indomitable urge to reproduce. From that perspective Bataille
stresses the difference between man and animals. Man is distinguished from animals by his ability to think ahead. He or she can
imagine a future goal. He or she works towards it, without deriving
immediate satisfaction from their labour. The capacity to pursue
goals in the future makes man see life as a project, something
animals cannot do. They know only immediate gratification of
needs and live according to their immediate impulses.

Man is distinguished from animals in another respect: he is
aware of his mortality. According to Bataille this makes man afraid

of death. Death is, in the light of all man's goal-oriented aspirations, a *scandal*, since death renders everything a man strives for futile. Dealing with death is bound by strict rules and prohibitions. What applies to death and dying also applies to the engendering of life. We human beings are aware of the fact that children may be created through sexual relations. Those children need protection, and society forbids sexual relations until there is a guarantee that any children can be brought into the world and grow up safely. Sex life is also hedged around with rules and forbidden. Eroticism – that is, sex geared to pleasure rather than reproduction – is distrusted or even criminalized, which also applies to masturbation.

These injunctions and prohibitions make death and sexuality seem rather gruesome and at the same time magical. For this special status Freud chose to use the term *taboo*, a word of Polynesian origin. Contrary to what is often thought, Freud sees taboos as very meaningful, since they guarantee the orderly continuation of a society and protect it from a descent into chaos, barbarism and bestiality.

Bataille also acknowledges the use of taboos, but for him there is something very special about the taboo: it is connected with what he calls *sovereignty*. Unlike man an animal has no fear of death and also no taboos. An animal satisfies its lust the moment it arises. Having no fear of death an animal dares to put its life on the line. Bataille observes that this means that the animal therefore always has complete control over its own actions. In that sense an animal is princely and has a sovereign will. Man does not have that sovereign will: he lost it at the same time as his consciousness came into being: human will is always subordinate to a future goal. But, Bataille observes, man has retained a deep-seated longing for animal sovereignty. We have a deep-rooted wish to do as we please, unhampered by rules, without having to account for the consequences of our actions. Moreover, we have a deep longing to look, like an animal, beyond the boundary of life without fear of death. Our longing for sovereignty is connected with our fear of death. If we give in to our fear of death, then we basically regain our lost sovereignty. But that death urge seeks an outlet at any cost. Within every ordered society taboos are broken: those are, for example, the moments when sex takes place without consideration of any children. Masturbation is therefore 'senseless' sexual behaviour for Bataille. It is a direct waste of energy, reserves, sperm and hence also life.

Bataille calls this wilful, wasteful crossing of boundaries 'transgression'. In that ecstasy of transgression man restores his lost sovereignty. In so doing he not only attains the highest achievement a man can imagine, but it also signals a regression to the animal state. So that the highest paradoxically equals the lowest. The ecstasy and excitement are therefore in Bataille's view followed by shame and guilt. Bataille's vision gives an insight into the centuries-old taboo against masturbation. According to his philosophy, masturbation is an animal act and also an infringement of the law.

Story of the Eye (1928), a product of his psychoanalysis, is a novella in which he makes the reader complicit in a series of criminal infringements of the law. In gruesome prose Bataille shows how the widening of boundaries almost automatically invokes a successive boundary, and how sexuality can turn violent. In thirteen short episodes a love triangle is described. This consists of a young male first-person narrator, his young female partner and a witness who acts as catalyst for the sexual transgressions. As the story proceeds the experiments become more frantic and more daring. This is a fragment from the episode 'Simone's confession and Sir Edmund's mass' (translated by Joachim Neugroschel). In the scene the young Simone goes to confession:

> One can readily imagine my stupor at watching Simone kneel down by the cabinet of the lugubrious confessor. While she confessed her sins, I waited, extremely anxious to see the outcome of such an unexpected action. I assumed this sordid

creature was going to burst from his booth, pounce upon this impious girl, and flagellate her. I was even getting ready to knock the dreadful phantom down and treat him to a few kicks; but nothing of the sort happened: the booth remained closed, Simone spoke on and on through the tiny grilled window, and that was all.

I was exchanging sharply interrogative looks with Sir Edmund when things began to grow clear: Simone was slowly scratching her thigh, moving her legs apart; keeping one knee on the prayer stool, she shifted one foot to the floor, and she was exposing more and more of her legs over her stockings while still murmuring her confession. At times she even seemed to be tossing off.

I softly drew up at the side to try to see what was happening: Simone really *was* masturbating, the left part of her face was pressed against the grille near the priest's head, her limbs tensed, her thighs splayed, her fingers rummaging deep in the fur; I was able to touch her, I bared her cunt for an instant. At that moment, I distinctly heard her say:

'Father, I have still not confessed the worst sin of all.'

A few seconds of silence.

'The worst sin of all is very simply that I'm tossing off while talking to you.'

More seconds of whispering inside, and finally almost aloud:

'If you don't believe me, I can show you.'

And indeed, Simone stood up and spread one thigh before the eye of the window while masturbating with a quick, sure hand.

'All right, priest,' cried Simone, banging away at the confessional, 'what are you doing in your shack there? Tossing off too?'

But the confessional kept its peace.

'Well, then I'll open.'

And Simone pulled out the door.

Inside, the visionary, standing there with lowered head, was mopping a sweat-bathed brow. The girl groped for his cock under the cassock: he didn't turn a hair. She pulled up the filthy black skirt so that the long cock stuck out, pink and hard: all he did was throw back his head with a grimace, and a hiss escaped through his teeth, but he didn't interfere with Simone, who shoved the bestiality into her mouth and took long sucks on it.

The priest is tortured to death, Sir Edmund cuts one of his eyes out, Simone inserts it in her vagina and the first-person narrator looks at it:

Now I stood up and, while Simone lay on her side, I drew her thighs apart, and found myself facing something I imagine I had been waiting for in the same way that a guillotine waits for neck to slice. I even felt as my eyes were bulging from my head, erectile with horror; in Simone's hairy vagina, I saw the wan blue eye of Marcelle, gazing at me through tears of urine. Streaks of come in the steaming hair helped give that dreamy vision a disastrous sadness. I held the thighs open while Simone was convulsed by the urinary spasm, and the burning urine streamed out from under the eye to the thighs below . . .

Story of the Eye is a horrific account. The dreamy atmosphere in which the events take place and the metaphorical game with the eye make it hard to read it as realistic pornography. In the succession of increasingly gruesome debauches one discerns an allegory: that of man's quest for the impossible.

Finally there are the views of the contemporary philosopher Michel Onfray (1959–). He is one of the few thinkers to write positively about masturbation. Onfray is French and a secondary schoolteacher, and a passionate advocate of hedonism: in his view the meaning of life consists in satisfying the senses, provided no harm is done to other people. His *Contre-histoire de la philosophie* is used as a text book in the senior years of secondary schools. It is a subjective, critical, non-conformist and anarchic book by a rebellious author, designed to teach young people to think critically about the big questions of life. One of the things Onfray argues for is masturbation. He writes: 'Masturbation is a natural phenomenon and its suppression is a cultural phenomenon. There are no good reasons for guilt feelings, or shame . . .' Enough said!

Conclusions

Most religious systems are exercises in detachment. True spirituality is abstraction from concrete, sensual desire. Sublimation may precede such an abstraction, but in fact stands apart from it; even Casanova sublimated his erotic practices in his stories. Masturbation comes closer to spirituality than sublimation. Auto-eroticism illustrates the religious rule of thumb that not doing is on a higher plane than doing. Masturbation is in fact the way to detachment; castration imposes it. For someone wishing to observe absolute celibacy, the second step follows from the first.

The odd thing is that in the Middle Ages sperm had a diabolical nature: demons were the product of sperm. After Anthoni van Leeuwenhoek's discovery of live spermatozoa with his microscope, a mechanistic view of sperm developed, but through Tissot it became mainly a substance from which both health and progeny sprang. Man as a machine was no longer enough. Men also became sperm banks, but those who with Plato regard man as a divine plant, rooted in the earth and burgeoning with desires, striving mightily to reach the boundless clarity above, have – in their own selves – the physical part too, to the point of ecstasy, and carried along by that ecstasy people can climb to a majestic height. Whatever other philosophers may think.

8

Writers and Poets

In fiction one can find many descriptions of sexual dissipation, but the topic of masturbation still remains a poor relation. The under-representation of the masturbation motif in literature is undoubtedly connected with the undeniably unspectacular character of this basically solitary activity. Everyone can do it, it offers few interesting variations and in itself it is not terribly exciting. The description of masturbating with a beefsteak is not so very original: decades ago, in *Portnoy's Complaint*, Philip Roth described using a piece of liver for the same purpose. Apart from that writers are mainly concerned with the feeling of shame involved. 'Because writing is a solitary activity,' the editor of a well-known publishing house said to me, 'they have relatively many opportunities to masturbate.' She is definitely on the right lines.

I went in search of masturbation in literature, which requires help. What better guide is there through the paradise of literary oblivion than Dutch author and former poet laureate Gerrit Komrij? He goes treasure-hunting, for example, in nineteenth-century hovels and the cellars of dusty libraries. It was a period awash with ink, an age of spewing presses and all kinds of rag paper. The result is called *Submerged Books*. In Komrij's book they are collected together from forgotten and lost libraries containing for example, *Charlot s'amuse*, the clinical-pathological novel on masturbation, so intriguing and compelling that we had to wait for *Portnoy's Complaint* to see the same theme dealt with so obsessively. There may be millions of human remains under the ground but another great army of coffins is found in the libraries above ground, like a spirit hovering above the bones. That is the cemetery of our past, the mortuary of knowledge, civilization, foolishness to which everyone has free access who has the magic wand with which one can bring the dead to life: literacy. A hushed, aristocratic library gives meaning to the whoosh of the senseless butcher's knife of world history.

The reader of these pages will see that the variation in masturbation as described in poetry and prose is found not so much in the techniques used as in the diversity of circumstance, locations, motives and opinions accompanying the phenomenon. Frank McCourt, for example, in *Angela's Ashes*, does it on a hill in view of a flock of sheep. It is clear that poetry and prose about masturbation can have a sobering effect on this one-person activity – but not necessarily. A woman fingering herself or a man jerking off can of course serve perfectly well as voyeuristic sex objects.

There are not many writers and poets whose work focuses on the phenomenon of masturbation itself. The Marquis de Sade, Marcel Proust, James Joyce and Jean Genet, among others, wrote primary masturbatory literature. I knew of very few female counterparts beforehand: only the medieval mystical poet Hadewych and the American poet Emily Dickinson. There were without doubt more, and that indeed proved to be the case, leaving me feeling a complete amateur. The chapter below reflects the beginnings of my modest exploration, no more. A young scholar could turn this into a full-scale investigation and write a thesis on the subject. My own urge to explore literature is entirely due to the passionate, infectious enthusiasm of a teacher at high school. We will start far back in time.

Classical texts

Anyone setting out hopefully in search of Classical texts on masturbation is in for a disappointment. In Classical literature there is plenty on sexuality, but solitary sex was obviously considered too intimate or too banal. In 1979 the East German Classicist Werner Krenkel gathered all the extant material together. He wrote an extensive article, mainly because he defined the subject in very broad terms, and also dealt with the visual arts. The literary material turned out to be limited and it was striking that all the higher literary genres such as epic, tragedy and historiography were conspicuous by their absence. Only a trawl through comedies, satires and epigrams produced any results.

This scarcity indicates that the Classical attitude to masturbation was in general not positive. With the Greeks appreciation could be described at its most favourable as 'neutral'; with the Romans it had negative connotations. Masturbation was mostly associated with the weaker members of society and slaves (Martial, *Epigram XI, 104*). Against this background it is interesting to examine Classical terminology for masturbation more closely. As stated in the introductory chapter, the word masturbation derives from Latin. Although the word probably existed earlier, it was the Roman poet Martial (*c.* AD 40–101) who is credited with the first recorded use of the word *masturbari*, in *Epigram IX, 41* (translated by George Augustus Sala):

> While you never indulge in a woman's embrace,
>> But rely on your whorish left hand,
> And call yourself chaste, yourself you debase
>> By a crime men can scarce understand.
> Horatius once fucked the delight of his home,
>> And three noble offspring she bore;
> And Mars lay but once with the mother of Rome,
>> And made one and one into four.

But if either of their fingers in lust had imbrued,
  Nor with these goodly ladies had lain,
Those happy results would never have accrued;
  So listen while I now explain,
What your fingers are recklessly throwing away
  Without stint or the least hesitation,
Is God's divine image, repeated in clay,
  Is man, our Lord's noblest creation!

The Latin text raises a few questions. Martial uses the usual term 'fuck' (*futuere*) and apart from that very current, everyday words. The exceptionally long word *masturbatus* ('having masturbated') stands out as quite unusual. It is a weighty, 'blustery' word, and in addition it is difficult to establish how far the poet is using his words seriously. Martial has a reputation as a flippant, sarcastic poet, but in the last lines the sentiments would do credit to a Roman Catholic divine. The examples of twins and triplets come from Roman mythology and may be either serious or ironic in intent. The Horatius mentioned here is not the celebrated writer, but the father of the three Horatii who fought the three Curiatii (Livy *I*, 24–6). 'The mother of Rome' refers to Ilia, who bore Romulus and Remus.

In the view of Werner Krenkel, Martial intended in this epigram not so much to contribute to sexual ethics but to nod ironically in the direction of the population policy of Emperor Domitian. The text need not therefore be taken too seriously, although it does certainly portray masturbation negatively. That also applies to another epigram of Martial's (*XI, 104*), in which Phrygian slaves secretly masturbate when they see Hector making love to his wife. In that case the long form of the single word *masturbabantur* fills the whole of the line up to the caesura. A Classicist I consulted suggested that the length of the word implied that the slaves spent the whole time happily masturbating.

The noun *masturbator* occurs in an epigram (*XIV, 203*) that served as a kind of gift tag for a slave girl: 'She moves her fanny in such a way and is so raunchy that it would turn even Hippolytus into a masturbator.' So, not even the legendarily chaste Hippolytus would be able control himself.

Epigram IX, 42 is also about masturbation and Romulus and Remus are mentioned in passing:

> You never sleep with a girl, your hand
> is both lover and sweet.
> The shame you fail to understand,
> your ignorance is complete.
> One spell in bed brought triplets to Horace
> and twins to the god of War:
> they were Romulus and Remus.
> All children you just abhor.
> Neither of us would even exist
> if our hands' sole daily work
> were in lonely, infamous joy to persist
> and we did nothing but jerk.
> Follow nature instead: it knew
> both its wishes and aim.
> What your hand now squanders like dew,
> is, Ponticus, a man without name.

Epigram XI, 73 reads as follows:

> You always swear 'I'll be there' when I ask you to
> and name the day and hour (a real red-letter day!)
> I lie and wait for hours till I can welcome you
> while impatient longing and lust with my feelings play.
> Until my hand, not you, extinguishes desire.
> So, Lygdus, should I now ask you one thing more?
> You with all your whims, go on, you silly liar,
> carry the sunshade for your cross-eyed grubby whore!

Apart from Martial the word 'masturbation' is not used anywhere in Roman literature. Nor is it used in medical or philosophical writings. It was not even the 'normal' word for auto-eroticism. *Fricare* (to rub) was the most common term, comparable with 'jerking off'. Other terms include *trusare* (to push), *tractare* (to pull) and the more euphemistic *fovere* (to cherish) and *tangere* (to touch).

Yet such words occur only sporadically. Most allusions are to hands and fingers, usually combined with an adjective. In the poem quoted above Ponticus used his left hand. The left side had a negative charge for the Romans. Other writers like Ovid and Lucilius (a satirist from the first century BC) were left-handed. The latter wrote the celebrated line *at laeva lacrimas muttoni absterget amica*, meaning 'his girlfriend wipes her tears from his prick with her left hand; she is crying because the masturbator is not satisfying her'. However, tears are also used to denote drops of sperm, which gives a different translation: 'with her left hand his girlfriend wipes the sperm from his prick'. My gut feeling tells me the second translation is the best.

As for most Romans, for Martial it was far better to find satisfaction with a woman or a slave than to indulge in masturbation. His tender and often moving poems on slave boys are unmistakable evidence of his own preference.

The same applied to the Ancient Greeks. This is clear from a poem by Skythinos (dates unknown). According to a poem in the *Greek Anthology*, masturbation was the last resort for the Greeks too:

Much woe, hellish strife and great fire came upon me:
Ilisos is full-grown and ready for loving.
Sixteen he is: what an age that is and how many
    little charms along with a great sweetness;
his voice is splendid when reading, more splendid still
his lips' kisses. Most splendid of all to have him completely.

'Just look,' he says; oh ye gods, in sleepless nights
I must jerk off because of this lover.

Another poem by Skythinos:

Now you've gone stiff, nameless one, now you're growing,
Expanding with your full charge, there's just no end to it.
But if Nemesenos interferes
to be of service to me you become a dead puppet.
Swell alone then, twitch and cry: it'll all be in vain,
Don't expect that my hand will spare you sweet pain.

Finally, the playwright Aristophanes gave the following sensible advice in his early drama *Women in the Assembly*:

then the women running to meet you in the crossroads will say, 'This way, come to our house, you will find a beautiful young girl there.' – 'And I,' another will call from her balcony, 'have one so pretty and as white as milk; but before touching her, you must sleep with me.' And the ugly men, watching closely after the handsome fellows, will say, 'Hi! friend, where are you running to? Go in, but you must do nothing; it's the ugly and the flat-nosed to whom the law gives the right to make love first; amuse yourself on the porch while you wait, in handling your fig-leaves and playing with yourself.'

French priapic verse of the sixteenth and seventeenth centuries

Masturbation – both male and female – is a common theme in sixteenth and seventeenth-century priapic verse. The genre derives its name from Priapus, a god from the Greek and Roman pantheon, a symbol of the erect penis, and comprises erotic poems in which physical aspects of love are central. There is no clear-cut poetic form like, for example, the sonnet. The label priapic refers to the content and the spirit of the content. But there is a basic difference between a smutty street song and a priapic poem!

Every French person with an above-average interest in literature knows that the great French authors wrote erotica. From the seventeenth century on collections of priapic poems were published and frequently reprinted in France. What's more scholars are still occupied in tracing priapic poems and identifying authors. The 'Certain abbé se manuélisait', is from *Contes et épigrammes libres* by Jean-Baptiste Rousseau (1671–1741):

> A certain abbot each day at dawn,
> in love with his neighbour, tugged hard at his rod.
> His confessor asked if such things were right:
> 'Your habit serves virtue. Can her beauty match God?'
> 'Ah!' said the abbot, no angel could nod
> at her, she's a wonder of love, she's first class,
> as white as lily, a wonderful arse,
> her tits and her crotch must have dropped from the sky.
> I think of her always and to my great shame
> even here I get horny.' Then came the reply:
> 'I'm sure that you do, for I feel just the same.'

The poet Maynard was not keen on masturbation for women:

> You beauty who love without a bloke,
> do you thrill when your own fingers stroke
> your little mons Veneris?
> Stop! What imperfect joy is this!

Sieur de Sigone, in his disappointment, gives up completely after a tryst with a skinny lady:

> First grow fairer, rounder in form,

otherwise say goodbye to sex . . .
And if hot lusts that spot still vex,
stick in your thumb to keep it warm.

And in *Le Parnasse Satyrique* we read:

Old man! A monster in my eyes,
who makes me live a life too calm,
you cannot make that member rise,
so you threaten me with lifted arm.
I tell you: until your tantrums cool
Keep your hand limp, just like your tool.

The poet broaches a problem that is still relevant in the twenty-first century: inequality of desire, lack of sexual fulfilment . . .

If the hand no longer suffices for masturbation, out comes the godemiché:

You make with leather, needle and thread
a sturdy penis with shaft and head
from one of your mother's old gloves.

In the view of the poet Motin, a godemiché remains a makeshift. In one of his priapic verses he has a courtesan, before she finally quits, giving away all her professional accoutrements to a very young successor. All she wants to keep is her godemiché, because:

What was she to do? You have choice galore,
of choice equipment to sate your lust, young whore;
it's a shame to give something to one who's richer than you!

The godemiché was popularly known as a 'chaplet' or a 'rosary', a name found in a poem by Viau:

When my prick grows and excitement calls
and a mule's prick in hardness it exceeds,
my love likes to fondle my two balls
better than her rosary beads!

As was discussed earlier godemichés were made of all kinds of materials. In a sonnet dedicated to the 'Précieuses', a nickname for the female members of seventeenth-century literary and artistic societies, Claude le Petit maintains that even a roll of paper can do excellent service:

And if this verse sets your body aflame,
roll this book till it's oblong, smooth and stiff.
Then it can serve as a godemiché.

The poet Maynard describes the crème de la crème among godemichés:

You thrust a glass instrument
deep into your body.

He is referring to a godemiché of Venetian glass, usually filled with warm water, or urine. The poet Ronsard also has his say on the matter. He laments apropos of a lover who in his eyes does not respond to him passionately enough:

I'm complaining, since she bought round here
a godemiché that her hand can steer,
with which she chastely wrecks her health each night.

Ronsard switches to the consequences of using an artificial penis:

Breath that stinks,
slime under which the bed almost sinks,

eyes hollow and ringed, skin pale and white,
from the false pleasure that grabs her each night.

This last quotation is very interesting, because Ronsard did not
believe in the fairy stories about the effects of masturbation. His
verses give him away: inwardly a heathen (if that word still means
anything), he nevertheless ultimately submits to the prevailing
morality.

Making fun of masturbation was certainly not a sinecure, but
meant taking a clear stand. It is no accident that in the medieval
books of penance there were more sections on masturbation than
on sodomy or bestiality. Yet in seventeenth-century priapic verse
the condemnation of masturbation is less frequent than its
opposite. Ronsard's judgement is rare, but even rarer is the sharp
dismissal of Claude d'Esternod:

We humans
have less reason than a beast:
a beast will never pollute itself.

As the reader knows, he had his facts wrong. Masturbation by
women is generally condemned in priapic verses, but mostly as
'unfair competition', since the poets were men! However, when it
comes to male masturbation they almost always tend to gloss over
the negative aspects. Take the poet Viau:

I was alone. A silly ass!
I made love to the blankets
And fucked my nightshirt, alas!

Or Sieur de la Porte:

But I bet you that our hero grand,
drunk on words loose and large,

will take his Member in his hand
and much to his relief – discharge.

The poet Baïf:

My hand, so obliging, can in both
cases do all the work.

That means making love without a woman and drinking without
a goblet . . . Maynard, who condemned masturbation by women,
took a nuanced view. He preferred coitus, but:

If she's not pretty and keen to play,
I'd sooner be comfortable any day
and lean on a post and jerk off.

To conclude this section, here is a warning in an epigram attributed to Maynard:

La Roche, when the tide is well-disposed
I'll come back soon for another look.
Till then I send you enclosed
Aretino's sexual position book.
But be careful, as you gaze
at the hundred positions and ways
in which man's reproduction is planned,
that your Sex doesn't grow as stiff as a bone
and it doesn't spurt right into your hand,
after your loved one has left you alone!

Male authors

The celebrated French writer and philosopher Jean-Jacques
Rousseau (1712–1778) was a friend of Tissot's and as an

Enlightenment thinker was profoundly influenced by the Calvinist physician. In his *Confessions* (translated by Angela Scholar) Rousseau describes his lone struggle against masturbation:

> I had learned to use that dangerous substitution which defrauds nature . . . This vice, so congenial to shame and timidity, is, in addition, very attractive to those of a lively imagination, for it places at their disposal, as it were, the whole of the other sex and makes any lovely woman that tempts them serve their desires without their needing to obtain her consent.

As a young man he had left Switzerland and travelled to Italy and stayed in a monastery there. One day he was shocked to find a priest masturbating right in front of him in church. It is possible that partly because of this he became a greater supporter of Tissot and as a European celebrity contributed to the huge sales of Tissot's books.

The reasoning of the Enlightenment was directed towards a clear aim: the creation of a perfect society. Rousseau began his *Social Contract* as follows: 'In this inquiry I shall endeavour always to unite what right sanctions with what is prescribed by interest, in order that justice and utility may in no case be divided' (translated by G.D.H. Cole). And in the area of sexuality and relationships that meant: 'The most ancient of all societies, and the only one that is natural, is the family.'

Sexuality in marriage was useful and usefulness was reasonable. There was no place for masturbation in such a scheme. In short, the struggle against masturbation was a logical consequence of the rationalist and utilitarian thinking of the Enlightenment.

It has been claimed that as a young man even Johann Wolfgang von Goethe (1749–1832) masturbated frequently, probably on the basis of a passage from his autobiography *Fiction and Truth*, describing student life in Leipzig. He loses his sweetheart there because, so he thinks, he has neglected her, and he describes how he takes out the loss on his own body:

> I had really lost her and the frenzy with which took I revenge on myself, attacking my physical nature in all kinds of absurd ways in order to do some harm to my moral nature, con-tributed greatly to the constitutional ills through which I lost the best years of my life; indeed, I might have succumbed completely to this loss had not poetic talent with its healing powers proved particularly useful.

Another, negative, reference is found in his *Venetian Epigrams* (translated by David Luke):

> 'Stranger-man, come, let's drink coffee!' she says,
>   and she means
> 'let me wank you'.
> So much for coffee, my friends; I've always hated the stuff.

Mark Twain (1835–1910), the American novelist best known for his classic tales *The Adventures of Tom Sawyer* and *The Adventures of Huckleberry Finn*, was a very committed writer and speaker, with outspoken anti-racist, anti-imperialist and anti-capitalist views. At the end of the nineteenth century – when the convic-tion that masturbation caused disease was at its height – Twain ridiculed it in a highly satirical treatment of the beneficial effects of the practice. This was a speech given in Paris in 1879 to the 'Stomach Club'. It was considered so offensive that it was published only 85 years later. This is an extract:

> Caesar, in his *Commentaries*, says, 'To the lonely it is company; to the forsaken it is a friend; to the aged and to the impotent it is a benefactor; they that are penniless are yet rich, in that they still have this majestic diversion.' In another place this

excellent observer has said, 'there are times when I prefer it to sodomy.'

Robinson Crusoe says, 'I cannot describe what I owe to this gentle art.'

Queen Elizabeth said, 'It is the bulwark of virginity.'

Cetewayo, the Zulu hero, remarked that, 'a jerk in the hand is worth two in the bush.'

The immortal Franklin has said, 'Masturbation is the mother of invention.' He also said, 'Masturbation is the best policy.'

Michelangelo and all the other old Masters — old Masters, I will remark, is an abbreviation, a contraction — have used similar language. Michelangelo said to Pope Julius II, 'Self-negation is noble, self-culture is beneficent, self-possession is manly, but to the truly great and inspiring soul they are poor and tame compared to self-abuse.'

Great men are quite often great sinners. When Maxim Gorky (1868–1936) asked his old colleague, the Christian convert Leo Tolstoy (1828–1910), the apostle of abstinence, if he had ever 'sinned' in his youth, Tolstoy's reply was, 'I should say so!' What applies to Augustine applies to Tolstoy: when they could no longer do it, they called it sin. They had enjoyed to the full what in later life they condemned . . . Perhaps in such cases there is a question of unconscious jealousy. Sexual decline makes people envious of the visible signs of vitality in young people whom these gentlemen 'caught in the act'.

Gorky dealt with masturbation in *The Life of Klim Samgin*. The novel's main character thinks about the horrifying book by Professor Tarnovski on the pernicious effects of masturbation, a book that his mother has passed on to him some time before as a precaution. Another renowned Russian writer, Nicolai Vasilyevich Gogol (1809–1852), whose works include *Diary of a Madman*, was a prolific masturbator, which undoubtedly influenced his melancholy humour.

Melancholy was also the dominant mood of the work of Scandinavian philosopher Søren Kierkegaard (1813–1855). While at university he met Regina Olsen, ten years his junior. Shortly after completing his studies Kierkegaard visited her at her parents' home. The visit resulted in an engagement, which was, however, was short-lived. Long afterwards, in his inner world and in his diary entries Regina continued to play a large, almost mythological role. Kierkegaard remained emotionally true to her until his death, as is shown by the fact that she was his sole heir.

The Swede August Strindberg (1849–1912) made his name as a playwright, but practised virtually every literary genre. In his first period Strindberg wrote mainly poetry, in which he opposed the late-Romantic movement and deliberately used non-poetic language. The content too reflects the militant tone of the years after 1880 and the urge towards innovation. In 1892 Strindberg became a bohemian, and wandered through Germany and France. In Paris he experienced a deep mental crisis, which led him to a new, undogmatic and non-denominational but Christian religious belief, in which guilt and penance remained prominent. In his autobiography he wrote about what masturbation had evoked in his youth:

Johan opened his satchel and took out the ghastly exercise book. His eyes scanned the pages and at first he did not dare to read exactly what was written. The blood drained from his face, the veins in his wrists were pounding – though he was only just approaching twenty-five. So was he already doomed or condemned to madness? His spine and brain would shrivel up, his face would become like a skull, his hair would fall out and his hands would start trembling – awful!

Despite this Strindberg was to write great works far into his old age. He was married five times and experienced the accompanying interpersonal ups and downs.

In *Ulysses* (1922) James Joyce (1882–1941) points an accusing finger at woman. In the notorious thirteenth chapter Leopold Bloom admonishes himself severely for having masturbated on the beach while leering at a young woman. But a few sentences later he calls her a 'hot little devil'. With that warning he places the responsibility at *her* feet and goes on to accuse her of witchcraft: she has sucked all the manliness out of him . . .

In *Journey to the End of the Night* (1932), the first novel of Louis-Ferdinand Céline (1894–1961), sex acts as a painkiller, a panacea against all evils. In 1934, when it appeared, the book was a bombshell. Today it is regarded as one of the high points of twentieth-century world literature. The whole novel is awash with free-and-easy sex, at a time when the masses were still kept in check by a suffocating morality. For Céline sex is a safety valve, an aspirin, an anti-depressive. He does not have a very high opinion of institutions like marriage and family. The *Voyage*, like the rest of Céline's work, is a romanticized autobiography. The book was a revelation; a doctor by training, Céline undermined the generally futile legislative approach of the Académie Française with his raw confessions. Like the late-medieval 'scoundrel' Rabelais, the author opts for vulgar vernacular speech, reinforced liberally with neologisms. His tone is quite unique: people shout, curse and swear to their heart's content. His work creates a kind of verbal delirium and puts the reader in a trance. His style has the hypnotic beauty of a poison snake and all the verbal violence has an unmistakably psychologically liberating effect.

Sexuality in Céline is very ambiguous. A mother masturbates as her child lies dying, and after the child dies she cannot stop . . . In Céline sex is free of all Christian value judgements, but does have a consistent diabolical quality. The book ends at daybreak, in the hope that everything will collapse, and that the Last Judgement is imminent.

World-renowned Swedish film director Ingmar Bergman (1918–2007), the son of a vicar, wrote in his autobiography of how

apprehensive he was about the possible punishment for masturbation. 'In the night before my first communion I strove with all
my might to defeat my demon. I wrestled with it until early in the
morning, but lost the battle. Jesus punished me with a gigantic
pustule in the middle of my pale forehead.'

The English poet Philip Larkin (1922–1985) eventually
restricted himself to masturbation ('Love again: wanking at ten
past three'). He had tentative relationships with women, but never
wanted to marry and disliked children. He defined sex as 'one of
those social activities that are quite alien to me, like playing
baccarat or doing the clog dance'. For most of his loveless life he
was, appropriately enough, the university librarian in 'dull Hull'.

The American writer John Kennedy Toole (1937–1969) describes in *A Confederacy of Dunces* how pleasant masturbation can
be. The novel is set in New Orleans and is the story of Ignatius J.
Reilly: an unforgettable, overweight, belching, Quixotic protagonist who intellectually terrorizes all around him. His insufferably
arrogant character, linked to an incredible aura of body odour surrounding him, has brought him little success in job applications.
And when he finally manages to fill a vacancy at Levy Pants, he
organizes a wildcat strike and is fired. He ends up as a hot-dog
seller. John Kennedy Toole committed suicide at the age of 32.
A Confederacy of Dunces finally appeared posthumously, thanks
to the efforts of the writer's mother. The book contains the following description of the hero's masturbation practices:

Ignatius touched the small erection that was pointing down-
ward into the sheet, held it, and lay still trying to decide what
to do. In this position, with the red flannel nightshirt around
his chest and his massive stomach sagging into the mattress,
he thought somewhat sadly that after eighteen years with his
hobby it had become merely a mechanical physical act
stripped of the flights of fancy and invention that he had
once been able to bring to it. At one time he had almost

developed it into an art form, practicing the hobby with the skill and fervor of an artist and philosopher, a scholar and a gentleman.

'You're a young man, yet you're completely bald, your face has gone to pieces and you have bags under your eyes, like an old man. And you have a paunch.' These are the words of the mother of a 35-year-old failed film director ('I') apropos of the special relationship he maintains with his sex organ ('he'). In *The Two of Us* the Italian writer and film director Alberto Moravia dissects with a cool, disciplined style man's inability to give his life a credible content. In a bizarre and rather impudent twist he has the director enter into a dialogue with his pig-headed penis, since the latter is constantly taking independent decisions and getting him into awkward situations. The novel (translated by Angus Davidson), which was made into a film in 1973, is hilarious:

> Tossed about by these slaps which hit him now from one side and now from the other, 'he' swung powerfully hither and thither and turned a dark, apoplectic red. I went on slapping Him with continued violence; but there now began to dawn on me the disconcerting feeling that he, masochist as he was, might actually be deriving some pleasure from the insults and blows. A few more slaps, a few abusive cries of 'scoundrel, scoundrel, scoundrel', the former delivered by a hand that became less and less precise and severe, the latter uttered by a voice that grew more and more hesitant and languid; and then suddenly, I felt that he was going to answer me.
>
> It was one of his usual answers, disloyal and treacherous, as I should have expected.

The narrator feels that ejaculation is unavoidable. Furious and in despair he tries to prevent it by bending and twisting the penis:

I wished the semen to return whence it had come, to be re-absorbed, to go back into its natural abode. Never, as at that moment in which 'he', in his crafty, underhand way, was making use of my very violence to make a fool of me and to unburden himself, never had I felt how sacred a thing semen is and how it is verily a sacrilege (a sacrilege which some desublimated persons are capable of committing, horrible as it is, as often as three times a day) to scatter it in order to pro-cure one moment of pleasure as fleeting as it is contemptible. Never had I felt this with such clarity as then, when 'he' was about to fling this sacred element – as thought it were spittle or some other insignificant secretion from a gland of no importance – upon the tiles of the bathroom floor.

I squeezed him, I tried to bend him and twist him; I twisted myself too, in a vain attempt to prevent the ejacula-tion, contracting the muscles of my abdomen and bending myself double; I turned swiftly round and hurled myself against the wash-basin, and then, just at the moment when I falsely believe I had been successful, just at that moment 'he' exploded in my hand like a newly uncorked bottle of sparkling wine. First there was a brief tremor, and a small quantity of semen, not more than a few drops, welled out at the tip. Then, as I was already hoping to escape with no more than this mod-est manifestation, the main part of the ejaculation suddenly flooded my hand, overflowing between my fingers, with which I was still trying to muffle and stifle my cunning adversary.

Overcome by acute despair, I let myself slip to the ground and, still squeezing him with frantic hatred, managed to roll, like an epileptic writhing in convulsions, across the floor to the hollow depression of the shower.

Atomised by the Frenchman Michel Houellebecq (1958–) is com-parable to Céline's *Voyage*. This book too is one long provocation. It is the story of the half-brothers Bruno and Michel, children of the same mother who grow up separately and meet only much later. The loner Michel grows into a brilliant molecular biologist, whose research will eventually lead to the replacement of *Homo sapiens* by a new, non-individualistic species. Bruno, who was tormented at school, becomes a sickly, sex-addicted hedonist. The book teems with scenes of masturbation or attempted masturbation. A few examples:

> Bruno jerked off at least three times a day. Here, he was surrounded by the vulvas of young women, sometimes less than three feet away, but Bruno realised they were closed to him: other boys were bigger, stronger, more tanned.

A little further on:

> Every Thursday afternoon Bruno would go to see Michel, taking the train from Crécy-la-Chapelle. If it was possible – and it almost always was – he would find a girl on her own and sit near her. Most of them wore see-through blouses or something similar and crossed their legs. He would not sit directly opposite, but at an angle, sometimes sharing the same seat a couple of feet away. He would get a hard-on the moment he saw the sweep of long blonde or dark hair. By the time he sat down, the throb in his underpants would be unbearable. He would take a handkerchief out of his pocket as he sat down and open a folder across his lap. In one or two tugs it was over. Sometimes, if the girl uncrossed her legs jus as he was taking his cock out, he didn't even need to touch himself; he came the moment he saw her knickers. The handkerchief was a back-up; he did not really need it. Usually he ejaculated across the folder, over pages of second degree equations, diagrams of insects, a graph of coal production in the USSR. The girl would carry on reading her magazine.

A quote about Michel:

> He himself masturbated rarely; his fantasies as a young research student, whether inspired by the Minitel, or by actual women (usually reps from large pharmaceutical companies), had gradually faded. Now he calmly observed the slow decline of his virility, relieved only by the occasional wank for which his 3 Suisses catalogue, supplemented now and then by a risqué CD-ROM (79FF) proved more than sufficient.

Later in the book there is a description of Bruno's experiences on the nudist beach at Cap d'Agde:

> The decorum among the men is even more striking further inland, above the line of the dunes. This is an area dedicated to amateurs of the *gang bang*, usually involving multiple male partners. Here, too, the germ is a couple who begin an intimate caress – commonly fellatio. Rapidly they find themselves surrounded by 10 or 20 single men. Sitting, standing or crouched on their haunches, they masturbate as they watch the scene. Often things go no further, the couple return to their embrace and the crowd slowly disperses. Sometimes the woman will gesture to indicate that she would like to masturbate, fellate or be penetrated by other men. In this case the men take it in turns – in no apparent hurry. When she wishes to stop, another simple gesture is sufficient. No words are exchanged; one can hear the wind whistling through the dunes, bowing the great tufts of coarse grass. Now and then, the wind dies away and the silence is almost total, broken only by cries of pleasure.
>
> It is not my intention to depict the naturist resort at Cap d'Agde as some sort of idyllic phalanstery out of Fourier. In Cap d'Agde, as anywhere, beautiful, firm young women and seductive virile men will find themselves inundated by

flattering propositions. In Cap d'Agde, as anywhere, the old and the ugly are condemned to masturbation – the sole difference being that whereas masturbation is generally prohibited in public, here it is looked upon with kindly compassion . . .

Bruno emerges as a hedonist, while his half-brother Michel could be described, with some exaggeration, as autistic. What links the two brothers is profound loneliness. Houellebecq seems to have a better grasp of Bruno than of the high-flying biologist Michel. Their loneliness is all the more poignant because the nineteenth-century naturalist explanations that Houellebecq gives the reader (the two are somehow predetermined by their parents and environment) do not work, at least not in the case of the real protagonist, Bruno. It is mainly because of present circumstances that he has turned out such an oppressed, limited, sexually warped figure, whose only desire and ability is actually to masturbate, that he seems to become 'magnified' before one's very eyes. Bruno becomes a 'man without qualities', representing late-twentieth-century *Homo sapiens*.

To my knowledge there is only one recent literary book that concentrates solely on male masturbation. This is *Spermatofolie* by Guillaume Cochin. The main character, Guillaume Cochin, has an unquenchable appetite for masturbation, which he indulges up to twelve times a day. He learned the habit as a boy and has simply continued. It is the only thing he is good at. He left school early and fails at a number of jobs. He, the 'Tiger Woods of masturbation', practises his talent in seclusion in a two-room flat, until he is accepted as a sperm donor. From being a red-haired, right-handed wanker he becomes a professional intermediary in the insemination process. Hurrah! Until after a year, halfway through the book, he is fired again. By then, however, the real damage has already been done. Twelve years later he turns out to have fathered 367 ginger-haired children, all carrying a genetic defect that will eventually result in blindness. Unless the father comes to the rescue, of course, which he dutifully does, but it is very doubtful whether this is enough to rescue the novel. The choice of theme, despite its absurdist enlargement, is too narrow in scope and reduces the characters to colourless puppets. The final resurrection of the flesh does little to alter that.

Female authors

The poet Emily Dickinson (1830–1886) was born in Massachusetts, and grew up in a peaceful Christian environment, with an authoritarian father and sick mother unapproachable for her children. The Dickinson family played a prominent role in political, cultural and religious life, but from an early age Emily withdrew and went her own way, choosing her own books. After spending a year at college she moved back into her parents' home. This was the beginning of a life of seclusion, dressed in white and extremely selective about the people she met. Although she never married she maintained a number of intimate friendships, including one with the married clergyman Charles Wadsworth, who in the view of many inspired her to write love poems, and with Thomas Wentworth Higginson, a leading literary figure to whom she sent a number of poems in her early twenties. He advised against publication, but immediately recognized the quality of her work. Ultimately only seven poems were published in Emily Dickinson's lifetime: when she died, at the age of 56, she left 1,775 poems, a number of which have been seen by some critics as evidence of auto-eroticism and/or lesbianism. Be that as it may, the sexiness of a poem like the one below is undeniable; it still impresses the reader with its electric intensity and compression, and powerful, visionary imagination:

> Wild Nights – Wild Nights!
> Were I with thee

Wild Nights should be
Our luxury!

Futile – the Winds –
To a Heart in port –
Done with the Compass –
Done with the Chart!

Rowing in Eden –
Ah, the Sea!
Might I but moor –Tonight –
In Thee!

In *The Leader of the Band* (1988), the writer Fay Weldon
(1931–) describes a married woman, consumed by lust for a married trumpeter and bandleader, who abandons her home and her
job to go on tour to France with her idol. Besides being presented
with fragmentary portraits and experiences of musicians, friends
male and female and relations, the reader is initiated into the
thoughts and opinions of the first-person narrator: a woman, oversexed, hard-bitten, coarse and pathetic, as is illustrated by passages
like this:

I couldn't bear it. My private parts still buzzed and zinged.
What had been replete and satisfied now hungered and
thirsted. The doves fluttered and pecked at my feet on the
powdered plaster, for spiders and weevils and all the things
Jack and I had disturbed. The birds seemed strangely tame and
not disconcerted in the least by the odd activity of humans. I
looked around for any possible source of satisfaction. It was
going to be hard to come by. The door handle seemed about
the right height, of cold, shocking metal. I took off my jeans
and rubbed myself up against it and, with the aid of my fingers,
came and came again, and cried out without shame, so the

doves rose and departed through a crack between the eaves and ceiling into somewhere less desperate and agitating. Then I felt better, as if I involved not just the organic world but the inorganic in the patterns of the changing universe. Drawn them in, united them. My flesh and cold metal had had business together and very right it seemed. Thank you, long Jack. Thank you, brass door handle.

The Greek writer Euridice (1964–) made her debut in 1990 with *F/32*. Ela, the book's heroine, has a wonderful and insatiable sex organ, which is inexhaustibly described. Eurydice knows no bounds in this cheerful postmodern fairy tale:

> She spends hours masturbating it [her cunt] to contentment, but masturbation increases her cunt's greed out of bounds; for whereas it might be satisfied by a few hours of straight fucking, it requires weeks of continual masturbation during which each new orgasm intensifies its lust. After some days, her pleasure becomes so quick and sharp that Ela starts over every few seconds. During these vicious cycles, she postpones all her other physical needs. Her ties with the world become dangerously severed. Her orgasms and fantasies stop only when a desperate enough man-in-love manages to break into her apartment and to cut through that charm circle of self-fucking which otherwise, Ela is convinced, would go on for ever.

Masturbation reminds Ela of the rivalry between the snake and the lemur; in the whole animal kingdom only these two are a match for each other. Caught in a fatal embrace their legendary battles last for days on end and it is never certain who is the winner until the moment of death. Men never show any understanding of Ela's struggle, and when it takes place in their presence they regard it as an exotic manifestation of Ela's extravagant sex drive. After the first jolt the sight of red-hot passion excites them. They try to help her, grabbing hold of her labia and attempting to smother the flame.

The début of the French novelist Alina Reyes (1956–), *The Butcher*, was quite rightly greeted by the critics with the sigh 'at last a book about happy sex'. A striking scene from the book is the one where at a certain moment the female protagonist quite spontaneously ties 'her' butcher to the legs of a table and a cupboard and then brings herself off provocatively right in his face.

A recent bestseller that dealt extensively with masturbation is *Wetlands* (1978) by the Germany-based English writer Charlotte Roche. In the first chapter the female protagonist Helen Memel tells us that she has suffered from haemorrhoids since childhood. Because she had damaged her anus while shaving herself, she will have to undergo an operation, in the course of which a bunch of haemorrhoids can also be removed. This is the start of a distasteful story of a bleeding anus, anal sex and especially masturbation. When Helen comes round from the anaesthetic, she realizes she has quite a wound down below. She is cared for by the male nurse Robin. At her request he takes photos of her opened anus, which looks horrific. Helen tells him about her experiences of anal sex (with or without chocodip: an unappetizing dessert containing faeces) and gives him a short lecture on how to avoid those chocodips with an anal douche. Helen dislikes the hygienic rules to which women are subjected by advertising in the magazines. Obviously women are not allowed to smell their crotch, which is why perfumed pads are marketed for their use. Helen hates these too. If you have oral sex with a man, you should be able to be just yourself, and hence stink. Anyway, she is crazy about her own bodily secretions. She stuffs snot, earwax, scabs, flakes of skin, sperm and smegma eagerly into her mouth.

The male nurse Robin reveals himself as a kind of knight in shining armour. However, Roche gives things a sexier slant by having her main character reflect on her great party piece: coming with just a prick in her arse and no other contact. Her habits are weird: she is so used to stuffing everything into her 'pussy', from avocado stones to complete showerheads. She also likes eating the scabs from her panties. In that area particularly Roche is endlessly creative. It always turns out that it can be a little dirtier. Not just working Dad's smart barbecue tongs inside to fish for a stray tampon, no, the tongs have to have the baked-on remains of meat and fat still on them.

Interviews with Charlotte Roche make it clear that she is out to break taboos. Taboos on sexuality, on the pressure on women to live as hygienically as possible, and the taboo on masturbation, though she has not yet succeeded in breaking the last of these.

More poems

Two of the most beautiful poems about masturbation are by women. In 'Against Coupling' the New Zealand poet Fleur Adcock (1934–) dismisses male-directed coitus and at the end of the poem proposes the only effective remedy against the swamp-like discomforts of copulation, namely masturbation. This is woman's revenge for two and a half thousand years of male monopoly *in eroticis*.

'The Ballad of the Sad Masturbator' by Anne Sexton, on the other hand, is more muted in tone and more elegiac than rebellious; the implication is that auto-eroticism is strictly second best, a poor consolation for a lost lover:

> The end of the affair is always death.
> She's my workshop. Slippery eye,
> out of the tribe of myself my breath
> finds you gone. I horrify
> I horrify those who stand by. I am fed.
> At night, alone, I marry the bed.

Finger to finger, now she's mine.
She's not too far. She's my encounter.
I beat her like a bell. I recline
in the bower where you used to mount her.
You borrowed me on the flowered spread.
At night, alone, I marry the bed.

Take for instance this night my love,
that every single couple puts together
with a joint overturning, beneath, above,
the abundant tow on sponge and feather,
kneeling and pushing head to head.
At night, alone, I marry the bed.

I break out of my body this way,
an annoying miracle. Could I
put the dream market on display?
I am spread out. I crucify.
My little plum is what you said.
At night, alone, I marry the bed.

Then my black-eyed rival came.
The lady of water, rising on the beach,
a piano at her finger tips, shame
on her lips and a flute's speech.
And I was the knock-kneed broom instead.
At night, alone, I marry the bed.

She took you the way a woman takes
a bargain dress off the rack
and I broke the way a stone breaks.
I give you back your books and fishing tack.
Today's paper says that you are wed.
At night, alone, I marry the bed.

The boys and girls are one tonight.
They unbutton blouses. They unzip flies.
They take off shoes. They turn off the light.
The glimmering creatures are full of lies.
They are eating each other. They are overfed.
At night, alone, I marry the bed.

Masturbation was and still is considered pathetic and unheroic, a pursuit for lonely wimps. Apart from that it is an unspectacular, solitary activity that anyone can engage in. In short, reading about people who masturbate is not normally very thrilling.

Having completed this chapter I discovered that the work of writers and poets does little or nothing to alleviate anxieties and concerns about masturbation, but unlike with doctors and theologians one does not find value judgements or a normative approach. Writers and poets undoubtedly have a broader, more human vision of reality.

9

Entertainment

Songs and limericks

Masturbation features in songs by such performers as Frank Zappa, Meat Loaf, Elton John and Elvis Costello ('Pump it up when you don't really need it, pump it up until you can feel it') and in 'Roll Yer Own' by Jethro Tull:

Roll yer own, roll it when there's something missing
and those wild cats howl, running in the moonshine.
Roll yer own if you can't buy readymade;
you won't be satisfied when you feel the sudden need
    to unwind.
Roll yer own: you got to hit that spot.
Roll yer own when your hands are hot.

And, for the older reader, in 'Sodomy Lyrics' from the musical *Hair*:

Sodomy
Fellatio
Cunnilingus
Pederasty

Father, why do these words sound so nasty?

Masturbation
Can be fun
Join the holy orgy
Kama Sutra
Everyone!

A limerick is a five-line verse form with a fairly tight metrical structure. In the first line a person or animal is introduced, mostly in conjunction with a place name. Lines 1, 2 and 5 rhyme with each other, as do the two shorter lines 3 and 4, producing the following rhyme scheme: AABBA. In addition a limerick often has a rather dubious content, and may even be downright crude. The last line is the punchline. After some detective work I managed to find a few on masturbation:

There's a quiet beach just north of LA
where I go to relax for a day.
As I lie in the sand
with my cock in my hand
I just stroke my stresses away.

and

An insatiable femme from Algiers
Loved to fondle small boys' chubby rears.
When finished with those,
she'd come using her toes,
and then douche herself with two beers.

There was a young lady named Bright
whose passions moved faster than light.
She set her dildo
to 'medium slow'
and creamed on the walls half the night.

Many more limericks, jokes and cartoons can be found, for example, in *The Solo Sex Joke Book* (1999) by Ralph Mead and Christian Snyder, and in *Rationale of the Dirty Joke* (1968) and in *The New Limerick* (1977) by G. Legman.

Films

I remember from my student days the time when Coca-Cola took legal action to prevent the release of the film *Alicia* (1974) by Wim Verstappen and Pim de la Parra. The film included a scene in which a girl masturbated with a litre-sized bottle of coke. Since then a large number of films have appeared featuring masturbation scenes. A search of the internet reveals the following top ten:

Adaptation
Being There
Amarcord
Bad Lieutenant
Mulholland Drive
But I'm a Cheerleader
The Squid and the Whale
Spanking the Monkey
Léolo
Fast Times at Ridgemont High

Connoisseurs and admirers of Meryl Streep should know that she is in *Adaptation*. She does not masturbate herself, but is the object of masturbatory fantasies. The same thing happens more or less in *It's Complicated* (2009). The ex-husband of Jane, played by Streep, is rung up just as he is about to masturbate so that the quality of his sperm can be assessed. It is not so much he as his new girlfriend who wants a child. The call comes not from her but from Jane. She invites her ex-husband for a cosy date . . . Her ex, played by Alec Baldwin, decides to save his sperm for her! The older reader may be interested in how Shirley MacLaine did 'it' in *Being There*! For further information, see http://blog.spout.com/2008/08/10-best-masturbation-scenes/.

The authors of the book *Erotic Cinema*, Douglas Keesey and Paul Duncan, devoted three pages to the phenomenon in film and add several marginal notes, for example, on what objects were used in what films in masturbation scenes. Again for real aficionados: a tree trunk in *Up!* (1976), a mechanical bull in *Urban Cowboy* (1980), a flute in *Lulu – Die Geschichte einer Frau* (1990), a spoon and a few earthworms in *A Real Young Girl* (1976), a showerhead in *Coming Soon* (1999), a floating doll for the bath in *Fessle mich!* (1990) and an orgasm machine in *Barbarella* (1968). In *Emmanuelle* (1974) it is just the hands, and similarly Kim Basinger uses no aids in *9½ Weeks* (1986). Masturbating nuns can be seen in, for example, *Interno di un Convento* (1977), *Immagini di un Convento* (1979) and *The Devils* (1971). In the first of these films a nun uses a godemiché with a picture of Jesus Christ on it, and in the last all the nuns start masturbating at the same moment.

In the film *Léolo* from 1992, Maxime Collin follows the literary example of Alex Portnoy in Philip Roth's novel, using a piece of raw liver to achieve sexual satisfaction. In *American Pie* (1999)

Masturbation in *Emmanuelle*.

Horny teenager Jim, played by Jason Biggs, comes in an apple pie (*American Pie*, 1999).

Jason Biggs uses one of his mother's freshly baked apple pies. To maximize the film's distribution, bowdlerized versions were issued.

Masturbation is sometimes presented very graphically, quite separately from romance, melancholy and desire, for example, in *Fast Times at Ridgemont High* (1982), in which a teenage girl is caught masturbating in the bath. In *There's Something About Mary* (1998) the main character, played by Ben Stiller, is caught by his co-lead Cameron Diaz, but denies it, after which he caresses her by spreading his ejaculate in her hair in the guise of 'gel'.

There is a quite humiliating scene in *Midnight Express* (1978) in which the convict played by Brad Davis jerks off quite openly when his girlfriend (Irene Miracle) is visiting and presses her breasts against the glass partition. And in *Ken Park* (2002) there are harrowing images of a teenager obsessed with death (James Ransome) who as he masturbates tries to strangle himself with a belt.

Of course there are also jokes about masturbation in films, for example in *The Apprenticeship of Duddy Kravitz* (1974), when the main character advises a fellow resident in his apartment block to masturbate with the right hand instead of the left because it may feel different, and then it will be 'sex with someone else'. I have previously quoted Woody Allen, who as Alvy Singer in *Annie Hall*

(1977) makes it clear that he has nothing against masturbation, since 'it's sex with someone I love'. A dialogue from *If You Don't Stop It . . . You'll Go Blind* (1978) describes a man who complains to the bartender about a fellow customer who has been fiddling with his willy while sitting next to him. 'Don't worry about it,' answers the bartender, to which the man retorts that the culprit had not used his own hand! In *The Brothers McMullen* (1995) one of the brothers sighs that 'if he masturbated as much as he wanted to, he would land in hospital full of guilt'.

The celebrated Danish filmmaker Lars von Trier (1953–) is the illustrious author of a number of extremely weird manifestos, including the most famous, 'Dogme 95', and 'I, Lars von Trier, am but a simple masturbator of the silver screen'. The first high point in his career was the so-called 'masturbation manifesto'. In 1991 at Cannes he walked off with the 'Grand Prix du Technique' for the visual steamroller which knocked spectators for six in their cinema seats! Each shot was constructed in an astonishing way, black-and-white and colour were used in tandem and there were numerous cameo appearances, including von Trier himself, as – believe it or not – a Jew, experiments with various lenses and colour filters, back and double projection, a narrator who almost falls asleep, both historical and political criticism and very impressive train symbolism.

After so much formal masturbation the incorrigible film-maker took a completely different tack in his Dogme 95 manifesto. In 2009 masturbation returned in the film *Antichrist*, where in one scene it is not sperm that is ejaculated but blood. Masturbation had happened previously in *Manderlay* (2005), by the protagonist Grace. During this scene a voiceover informs us, for example, that 'she lost all sense of morality and the heat surged through her loins', and 'who knows where this could have led, if she had not been disturbed'. I bet it would have led to an orgasm. Oh dear, it was meant to be ironic. Not everything by von Trier is a revelation.

It will be clear after this exploratory survey that masturbation has penetrated the non-pornographic film industry too, in the wake of *Emmanuelle*, which quite unexpectedly, thanks to the performance of Sylvia Kristel, became a huge success.

10

Artists

The work of almost every visual artist contains erotic images, in many cases confined to the intimate medium of drawing. Sometimes the artist causes indignation by deliberately overstepping the bounds of decency, as in the case of masturbation. A recent example is Czech artist David Cerny, who had been commissioned to produce a work of art for the European Council building in Brussels. The work depicts Europe as a model construction kit of EU countries. The artist has incorporated many jokes and pranks in the piece: the Netherlands is flooded, and only a few minarets still have their tops above water, while Bulgaria is nothing but a squatting-style toilet and in Italy players are masturbating with a ball. It provoked a storm of reactions!

True art-lovers will admit that art can only exist by virtue of taboos and that those taboos must be broken. Which artists have tried to break the taboo on masturbation?

I began my search by studying the bottom panel of Hieronymus Bosch's *Garden of Earthly Delights* for a whole evening. These days you can do that on the internet, and all the images can be enlarged. I drew a blank – there wasn't a single masturbator – and subsequently tried to make contact with respected art connoisseurs. I was unsuccessful, undoubtedly because the subject was not of immediate interest to them, though they didn't put it like that.

It also emerged that there were no art-historical textbooks on the topic, though there were of course on eroticism in art, but

Attic cup, 'Masturbating
Haetera', from the studio of
Nicosthenes, second half of
the 6th century BC.

these offered only dribs and drabs of relevant information. Ultimately old sexological works turned out to be the prime source.
The illustrations put me on the track of the artists below. What did
I find? In antiquity depictions of masturbation are fairly rare. And
if a depiction does turn up, it is of a satyr or of women, painted on
vases or walls. According to Hans Licht (1926, p. 24) there is a fine
vase painting in Brussels of a masturbating boy, but I was unable
to trace the vase. I did, though, find a depiction of a naked young
woman clutching an artificial penis ('olisbos') in each hand. She is
sitting with her legs wide apart: she is inserting one olisbos into
her clearly depicted vulva and is raising the other to her eager,
half-opened mouth.

The striking thing is that although the Greeks were only too
familiar with the central function of the clitoris in sexual pleasure,
the paintings create the impression that women made extensive
use of artificial penises. The satirist Lucian (AD 120–180) devoted
a dialogue to the subject in *Dialogues of the Courtesans,* in which
one haetera or courtesan tries to get her friend to reveal the name
of the master leather-worker, 'who produces such high-quality
goods'. It would, however, be wrong to assume that the olisbos was
used only by haeteras or lesbians. We can safely assume that the

artificial penis was a much-loved and widely used instrument even in ordinary women's chambers.

It is not until the dawning of the Enlightenment that masturbation is highlighted more often. That is when the story of masturbation in art begins in earnest.

Giorgione

The *Sleeping Venus* by Giorgione (1477–1510), also known as the Dresden Madonna, was taken to Dresden in 1697 and remained there until the end of the Second World War. For reasons of safety the painting had been taken to a depository, where the Russians discovered it and transported it to Moscow. In 1955 the painting returned to Dresden, since when it has hung in the Gemäldegalerie Alte Meister.

It shows the goddess Venus lying asleep on the edge of a clearing in the woods. The work admits of many interpretations, in which nature is usually central. Art historians, for example, point out that 'the outline of her body follows the shape of the hilly landscape in the background'.

Giorgione, *Sleeping Venus*, 1510, oil on canvas.

Venus' pose is linked to a woodcut from the fifteenth-century novel *Hypnerotomachia Poliphili*, which today is attributed to Francesco Colonna, and describes Poliphilius' search for his beloved Polia. Via woods, valleys and tortuous paths Poliphilius arrives at an island dedicated to Venus, where the appearance of the goddess herself seals the love between himself and Polia. In the painting the sleeping nymph is lying on a sheet. The caption to the painting reads: 'Mother of All Things', which at the time may have been a reference to the mother-goddess of nature, 'Venus genetrix'. The *Sleeping Venus* is also sometimes linked to the model 'Venus pudica' from antiquity.

In 1697 a certain Michiel wrote about a canvas showing a naked Venus sleeping in a landscape with a Cupid by Zorzo de Castelfranco (Giorgione), but according to him both the landscape and Cupid were completed by Titian. The latter, he claimed, had changed Giorgione's views on the painting. 'By painting sheets around the Venus, Titian had wanted to weaken the total identification of the woman with nature and by the addition of Amor had included a far from metaphorical allusion to sexuality in the painting,' wrote Michiel. Both features can be found in Titian's 'own' *Venus of Urbino*.

Both a good and bad attitude to sex begins with looking. Nudity forces the viewer to make a fundamental choice. Does he or she look at the other as a person or as an object? Everyone is familiar with the experience of looking in at a window and unexpectedly seeing a naked woman who is unaware that she is being looked at. You then have the choice: either you see her as a person and you look away, because you must respect her privacy, or you see her as an object and look closer. Most painters and sculptors, not only Classical but also modern, are aware of this choice and guide us in the right direction. Giorgione, for example, clearly depicts his Venus as a beautiful woman. He painted her in such a way that the focus is on her as a whole entity. He made her beauty a subject for reflection. The painting is definitely not pornographic. Porn directs the eyes to certain anatomical parts and puts the focus on woman as object. In fact it is not nudity that is pornographic, but the way of looking at it.

Titian

Titian (1487–1576) painted various Venuses during his lifetime, of which the most famous is the *Venus of Urbino*, probably produced in 1538 for Guidobaldo della Rovere, who became Duke of Urbino in that year. After the male line of the Della Roveres died out their art collection found its way to Florence, where the picture can still be seen.

The painting shows a naked young woman on a bed. In her right hand she holds a bouquet of roses, while her left hand rests on her mons Veneris, with the fingers on the clitoris. At the foot of the bed a young dog is asleep. In the background are two women who are rummaging in a chest, obviously hunting for Venus' clothes.

The most common art-historical interpretation of this painting is a Venus as a model of domestic virtue, on the grounds that the attributes by which the goddess of love is surrounded are depicted as an icon of marriage. The floral motifs in the painting particularly, the roses and the blueberry bush in the window, are seen as supporting this interpretation, while the puppy at Venus' feet is arguably a symbol of marital faithfulness. The woman herself, because of the domestic setting, could be a representation of the ideal wife. Well . . .

Art historians who are less convinced of the mythological identity of the lady in the picture and the two women behind her, call her a Venetian courtesan. This debate is quoted, for example, in *La vie quotidienne* by Paul Larivaille. She is probably a *cortigiana onesta*, one of Venice's higher-ranked courtesans.

The pose of the *Venus of Urbino* seems to have been taken directly from Giorgione's *Sleeping Venus*, but the context in which each goddess is placed is completely different. Whereas Giorgione's Venus is in nature and has closed her eyes, Titian's is lying on the bed of a luxurious chamber reminiscent of a Renaissance palace. She seems to be looking at the viewer. Titian's Venus is also wearing precious jewels: a bracelet round her right wrist, a pearl earring in her left ear and a ring on her left little finger. Her hair has been carefully arranged with braids. Giorgione's Venus has no such personal ornamentation and her hair falls naturally over her body.

What in my view is absent from virtually all art-historical interpretations is the significance of the position of the left hand. That applies to both Giorgione's and Titian's Venus. One thing is certain: both works of art were designed to be hung in the private chambers of senior figures at court. In her *Solitary Pleasures* the art historian Kelly Dennis writes about female sexuality in relation to these two paintings. In her view the previously quoted American writer and freethinker Mark Twain gives a completely different interpretation in *A Tramp Abroad*, a travelogue from 1880. He described the *Venus of Urbino* ironically as 'the filthiest and most obscene he had ever seen', because of 'the attitude of one of her arms and hand'. For him there was no doubt that she was masturbating. Kelly Dennis also comments that the *Venus*, precisely because it was intended for a private apartment, may be considered as pornographic. 'Nothing would have prevented the owner from starting to masturbate while looking at the Venus. In fact the person commissioning the painting called it simply a 'nude', that was all.

To cut a long story short: according to Kelly it is only recently that art historians have begun to accept the view that both this Venus and Giorgione's are examples of auto-eroticism, a general term for masturbation.

Rembrandt

On a recent visit to the Hermitage in St Petersburg I saw among the huge collection a magnificent etching by Rembrandt van Rijn (1609–1669) showing a male nude seated in front of a curtain. The man is definitely masturbating, and one can see how much he is enjoying it. In the art-historical literature we are told about an 'academic pose in a classic position expressing balance and harmony'. What balderdash! Even modern sex education manuals refer to this etching.

Rembrandt also depicted a masturbating woman. In this drawing the hand has a completely different function than that of a *cache-sexe*. The tension in the left forearm – in contrast to the relaxed right arm – points to masturbation. The drawing seems to be inspired by Titian's Venus – and at a time when witches were burnt at the stake for having had sexual relations with the devil.

Rembrandt's graphic work is of inestimable value as an erotic historical document. He shows very precisely the limits of

Rembrandt van Rijn, *Seated Male Nude*, c. 1646, etching.

Rembrandt van Rijn, *Nude Woman, Lying on a Cushion*, *c.* 1661, drawing.

contemporary tolerance. True, it was greater than one might expect on the basis of the official attitude of the Calvinist state Church, but still considerably less than in the Burgundian period.

Baudouin

Pierre Antoine Baudouin (1723–1769) worked mainly in gouache and preferred to paint scenes from social life. He was commissioned by the Marquise de Pompadour, one of his admirers, to paint miniatures for the Chapelle du Roi in Versailles. However,

Pierre Antoine Baudouin,
Le Midi, 18th-century gouache.

his illustrations *A Priest Teaches Young Girls their Catechism* and *The Confessional* had to be removed after the opening of the new royal place of worship because the archbishop of Paris was offended by them.

The same thing happened with *Le Midi*, in which an elegant young woman has been reading a book in a rococo summerhouse. She has dropped the book and is feeling cautiously under her skirt for her private parts . . .

Rops

Félicien Joseph Victor Rops (1833–1898) was a Belgian graphic artist, painter and caricaturist. His vision has satanic and pornographic undertones. His work (the kind of women he was fond of depicting were called *Ropsiennes* even during his lifetime) is no longer widely known. However, thirty years ago his work experienced a revival when there was a sudden surge of interest in Western Europe for the libertine precursors of the current liberal ethos. In Rops' vision woman was both earthy and part of paradise,

Félicien Joseph Victor Rops,
L'Idole, 1882.

partly the powerful and seductive woman, partly the woman driven by physical urges. The artist broke taboos by depicting the naked body without scruples, which in his day was very daring.

Rops was keen to taunt the Church. He alluded to the hypocrisy of some Christian virtues which outlawed nakedness but did allow naked divine figures in human form. His female figures, who personify seduction and evil, are generally modelled on Flemish girls with whom Rops was besotted.

In *Geschichten der Erotischen Kunst* by Eduard Fuchs I found a very unusual nude by Rops: a woman is climbing a phallic totem pole, the middle one of three. The impression is created that the woman is scaling the crucified Christ, but it is actually the devil. Though that fact was capable of enchanting liberal spirits in the 1970s, today no one finds it really exciting any longer. Now that he has lost his excitement, Rops can be seen as a more or less 'ordinary' artist, in whom we are immediately struck by his obsessive view of relations between men and women.

Félicien Rops liked short but intense stimuli and was unable to enter into long-term relationships. He deliberately chose non-professional models, since the latter would take him towards the classic, distanced nude. No, Rops wanted sex with everything, and always with a vitriolic undertone.

Klimt

Gustav Klimt (1862–1918) painted women in an introverted world, into which the outsider, the man, peers with excitement or fascination. The legs are pulled right up, the thighs pressed against the hips, the knees come up to the armpits. This self-absorbed masturbating woman doesn't want a scandal.

'Klimt', writes Gottfried Fliedl in his book *Klimt*, 'was interested precisely in the depersonalization of the sexually active woman. When Klimt draws a female nude, he emphasises the genitalia in an unmistakable way.' However, a few biographers

Gustav Klimt, *Seated Semi-nude with Closed Eyes*, 1913, pencil drawing.

describe how he usually received his models: dressed only in a monk's habit in a luxurious studio filled with exotic vapours. Strictly for the atmosphere, of course!

Times change. In Vienna around 1900 death and sex were regarded as symptoms of disorder. Both were taboo, and for that reason they provoked personal revolt. Gustav Klimt opted for passion, rebellion, life lived at fever pitch and angst. He asked himself what human beings really know about their fate. Klimt's work is imbued with the symbol of rebellion against the tyranny of materialism. Seductive wrappings hide sex in all its directness. The frequent use of gold in his work operates as a fig-leaf, since gold is treated as a non-colour.

De Feure

Georges Joseph van Sluyters (1868–1929), of Dutch origin, who gained fame as a painter under the name Georges de Feure, was one of the most original and versatile representatives of the fin de siècle. Initially he worked as a craftsman in a bookbinder's in The

Georges de Feure, *The Voice of Evil*, 1895, oil on panel.

Hague. It was here that he encountered Symbolism and in 1891 he decided to move to Paris, where he began his artistic career as an actor and poster designer, before making a name for himself as a painter of landscapes and women.

Besides painting he was active in all conceivable areas of applied art. He designed furniture, porcelain, jewellery, glassware and posters, and illustrated books. A pronounced feminine atmosphere is typical of his work.

The mysterious sphinx or the ambivalent young woman are not the only favoured female types in art nouveau: many fin-de-siècle artists feature woman as a downright malevolent figure and man plunging to his destruction.

The purely decorative style is as striking as the air of perversity that the woman exudes. The androgynous-looking female seems to have dark plans. The title, more than the work itself, testifies to the Puritanism of the age. Evil was above all sexual in nature. The woman in the painting is attracted by lesbian love: the voice of evil. She is looking at the two women lying in the background, one of whom has just had an orgasm. One can easily guess where the hand of the woman in the foreground is.

Beardsley

In Greek antiquity Lysistrata, the eponymous heroine of Aristophanes' play, persuades women to deny men their sexual pleasures. The women's aim in taking, or rather not taking, action was to end the Peloponnesian war. Lysistrata, tired of the endless squabbling between Athens and Sparta, committed her own body to the struggle for peace.

The idea of sexual abstinence as a political lever is inextricably linked to this Classical Greek comedy. Everyone knows that it did no good. In his play Aristophanes is far from flattering about these women, but it was a creative way to pillory the endless war. His conception continues to appeal to the imagination.

Aubrey Beardsley (1871–1898) was an influential artist. Typical features of his work are the powerful composition with sweeping lines and the strong contrast between light and shadow. This illustrated how greatly the artist's work was influenced by the

Aubrey Beardsley, illustration for an edition of Aristophanes' *Lysistrata*, 1896.

Japanese coloured woodcuts that were widely available at the time. Beardsley was diagnosed with TB as early as the age of seven, which is seen as a possible explanation for his unbridled creativity and his premature death.

Schoff

The graphic artist Otto Schoff (1888–1938) was an autodidact. In 1913 he went to Paris, at the time an artistic Mecca, and became friends with George Grosz and Herbert Fiedler. All drew nude sketches in the Académie Colarossi, which was extremely famous at the time. Countless pencil sketches bear witness to his fascination with nude models and talent as a draughtsman.

Much of his largely erotic art is included in the famous series *Lexicon Kulturgeschichte, Literatur und Kunst, Sexualwissenschaft: herausgegeben vom Institut für Sexualforschung*. Schoff ended his artistic career in Berlin.

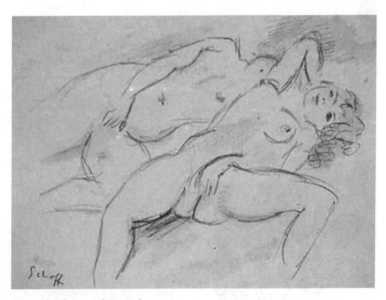

Otto Schoff, *Recumbent Girls*, c. 1920.

Egon Schiele, *Standing Woman in Red*, 1913, oils.

Schiele

Egon Schiele (1890–1918) is often mentioned in the same breath as his colleague Klimt. He died young of Spanish influenza. I read somewhere that in the last year of his life over six hundred models passed through Schiele's studio, which produced many times that number of drawings. We know that he picked up these models, sometimes literally, from the street, or the gutter. It's clear that he did not ask them for their passports, but he must have had an inkling that some of them were not much more than twelve years old.

Schiele rescued life drawing from academic hypocrisy and as he drew had his models masturbate shamelessly. He often stood on a ladder in order to achieve strange perspectives. His 'angles' were extraordinary in all respects! In the self-portrait *Eros* and *Self-Portrait, Masturbation, Shrouded in Black Drapery* Schiele showed himself completely absorbed in his own pleasure, excluding any physical and emotional relationship with the other. They are not

Egon Schiele, *Self-portrait, Masturbating, Shrouded in Black Drapery*, 1911.

beautiful paintings; their main raison d'être is their breaking of taboos at a time when it was still thought that masturbation caused blindness, mental illness and other horrors.

Grosz

German artist George Grosz (1893–1959) studied at the Dresden Art Academy from 1900 to 1912 and attended the School of Applied Art in Berlin. While still a student he published satirical cartoons in magazines and newspapers, and later founded the Club Dada artists' group. His work was controversial and in 1928 earned him a conviction for blasphemy.

With Two Women is a well-known watercolour in which one of the women is masturbating with a dildo. Many men find it intimidating and shocking.

In 1931 George Grosz settled in the United States and became lecturer at the Art Students League in New York. After the Nazis took power in Germany, Grosz's work was considered 'degenerate art' by them.

George Grosz, *With Two Women*, c. 1920, watercolour.

Schad

The work of German artist Christian Schad (1894–1982) is alienating, showing, for example, women fingering themselves without any mutual contact. It is irritating and at the same time mysterious, or is it porn? Is it connected with men's insatiable curiosity about women's experience of sex?

His art is elusive, but why? At first sight many portraits are just examples of figurative art, though they are unreal and chilly. He is

Christian Schad, *Girlfriends*, 1930, oils.

one of the iconic representatives of what is called in painting the New Objectivity – a reaction to 'chaotic' Expressionism.

The cool portraits of actresses, intellectuals and circus performers give a striking picture of a loveless period. Sometimes Schad abandons his chilly detachment and we find that true love is after all possible – especially where his own women are concerned. In 1929, for example, he paints his girlfriend Maika in Paris (*Halbnackt*). The young woman lies languidly among the cushions. Her pretty face and dark hair attract the attention, but so do her breasts, which are almost tangible in their fragile softness. As a German art historian once wrote of him: 'No painter of his time could paint skin in such a transparent and vulnerable way, the translucent network of the tiniest veins, saturated with intense sensuality.' The same kind of affection is expressed in the portraits of his second wife, Bettina Mittelstädt, whom he painted in 1942 and again in 1946. In that period Schad settled in Aschaffenburg, where he was to remain until his death.

Dalí

No survey of masturbation in modern art is complete without Salvador Dalí (1904–1989). The title of his painting *The Great Masturbator* is designed first and foremost to provoke. In the picture

Salvador Dalí, *The Great Masturbator*, 1929, oils.

the heroine appears to be preparing to perform fellatio. 'Of all the beauties of the human body,' Dalí wrote, 'it is the balls that exert the greatest influence on me. When I look at them, a supernatural ecstasy takes hold of me. My teacher Pujols said that they are the reservoir of uncreated beings.' In this way both Dalí and his teacher find their way to Judaic theology.

'But,' said Dalí, 'I really dislike balls that hang there limply, like empty bags. As far as I'm concerned they must be filled, firm, round and hard as a double mussel.'

Dalí also wrote: 'Painting, like love, works through the eyes and flows out again through the hairs of the paintbrush. My erotic delirium forces me to push my sodomist tendencies to a climax.'

Fischl

The painting by Eric Fischl (1948–), *Sleepwalker*, shows a boy masturbating into a plastic basin, in front of his parents' empty deckchairs. The illustration below is a preliminary study. At first sight it seems a pathetic spectacle, but the boy's enthusiastic keenness conveys the astonishing awareness that the painting is actually about power: the original, explosive power of being able

Eric Fischl, *Study for Sleepwalker*, 1979, oils.

to give oneself pleasure. The boy discovers this. As he painted Fischl was filled with the boy's feelings – pleasure mixed with anxiety about the painful humiliation to which he exposing himself as an artist. The painting was obviously broaching a taboo, but in the 1970s it still struck people as obscene.

Serrano

Andres Serrano (1950–), a controversial sex photographer, was born in New York and brought up as a Catholic. He trained at a very prestigious institution, the Brooklyn Museum Art School. The Brooklyn Museum of Art, of which the school forms part, is the second largest museum in New York State, with a collection of over a million and a half works of art embracing the whole history of art. The subjects that Serrano chooses often produce very raw images, but the artist indicates that there is scope to see beauty and tenderness in the less attractive aspects of life.

A portion of his photographs show extreme sexual acts, but Serrano manages to raise the subject above all vulgarity. One of his finest works shows a man performing fellatio on himself.

Down to the present Serrano has occupied himself with the question of what images the human eye can bear. With his shocking photos he is exploring what modern man still experiences as taboo.

Andres Serrano, *Auto Erotic*, 1996.

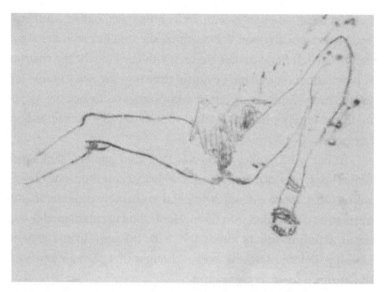

Tracey Emin, *Suffer Love II*, 2009, monoprint on paper, 21 x 29.6 cm.

Emin

Tracey Emin (1963–), who grew up in Margate on the Kent coast of England, shares the pleasure of her intimate female world with a large public. She invites us to pore over her daily life in minute detail. The critic Rudi Fuchs pointed out that her drawings are a kind of shorthand, which is a consequence of the way they are produced. The process is as follows: first, a thin, even coat of tough, sticky ink is applied to a glass plate. The artist then places a sheet of paper over it and with a tough pencil she draws very fast, in just a few movements, the motif, more or less as it has come into her mind. So that when the sheet of paper is then pulled off the tacky layer of ink, the mirror-image imprint of the drawing is left on the front. In the critic's view it has to be this fast because Emin wants to communicate honestly and at the same time in definitive form the memories by which she is haunted. There can be no doubt of this. The imprint of the ink is fragile and recalcitrant. The printed lines are scarce, and in the printing process stains remain.

What can one see? A woman leaning back, naked, with legs wide apart and an open vulva, which she touches with her right hand. The left hand makes contact with the clitoris: the realism is poignant and desolate. Beautiful drawings are not suitable for what Tracey Emin is trying to communicate. In her life sex is mainly a purely physical matter; something that is *inflicted* on her body.

'In her work Tracey Emin has found an effective language', writes the same critic, 'which enables her to communicate observations that are so disconcerting and vulnerably intimate that it hurts to be confronted with them. Her feeling is unfathomable but never maudlin; that is impossible with this raw, brittle way of working. Before I saw this work, I thought that photography was the medium for extreme realism.'

'But Tracey Emin's drawings, that spare, slippery way of drawing, make me see that photos generally suffer too much from what I could call atmosphere and additional work in the margin, which is too much of a distraction. There are no distractions in the drawings, they are so bare and abbreviated and you often have to search for exactly what it is you are seeing. This means that they simply cannot be coarse and vulgar. Whether they are beautiful or not is not the issue. Their feeling is true: you can either feel that and believe it or you can't.'

McKenzie

The artist Jordan McKenzie (1967–) covered 55 canvases with his sperm and then sprinkled them with charcoal. In this way his precious sperm was saved forever for posterity. His works were shown for a month at a London gallery. The vicar of a church in nearby Clerkenwell was very upset about it. 'All we can do is pray for the man. He is obvious a seriously disturbed person. It's unbelievable that someone should regard this as art and allow this monstrosity to be seen in his gallery.'

Jordan McKenzie, *Ejaculation Diary*, 2007.

The vicar was not the only one who disliked this art of ejacu-lation. Fellow-artist David Gleeson also found it disgusting. 'Of course, we had Tracey Emin displaying her panties, but this is of a completely different order. I am for every form of expression, but please, don't masturbate over a piece of paper.'

McKenzie was completely unperturbed by the criticism. He went further and promised to produce ejaculatory art three times a week from then on. 'I see it as a diary of my ejaculations, that is, totally sincere and delicate. I hope that people will carry on com-ing to look.'

McKenzie, though, was not the first to use sperm for his paint-ings; Andy Warhol 'beat' him to it. In painting his penis canvases he mixed the paint with a combination of urine and sperm. Even more outlandish mixtures are possible. In one of his literary-journalistic reports the writer Arnon Grunberg (1971–) relates how Muslim prisoners in Guantánamo Bay attacked their guards with a cocktail of faeces, urine, blood and sperm. Grunberg makes the following observation: 'One might assume that a reli-gious prisoner would preferably not masturbate, but Colonel

Tucker of the US Army confirmed by email that the cocktail used against the guards also contained sperm. In the past year this cocktail has been thrown over guards more than four hundred and thirty times.'

Summing up, one could argue on the basis of the above brief exploration that masturbation has been only sporadically depicted by visual artists, not only in Classical antiquity but even in the post-Enlightenment era. Perhaps they find it less interesting than writers and poets because they have to represent it both literally and figuratively. In contrast to writers and poets it is very rare for a visual artist to relate masturbation to himself or herself. It is even more difficult for purely visual artists like ballet dancers. To my knowledge there is only one ballet in which masturbation is depicted, namely *L'après-midi d'un faune*. It tells the story of a fawn that in the blistering midday heat of Sicily spies on two naked nymphs. It contains successive scenes in which the fawn's desires and dreams are expressed in the afternoon heat. Worn out with pursuing the nymphs, who flee in fear, the fawn finally gives in to an overwhelming sleep, in which his dreams of domination over Universal Nature come true.

The ballet was first performed in Paris in 1912 and caused a scandal. It had been choreographed by the dancer Vaslav Nijinsky (1889–1950), to the music of Claude Debussy (1862–1918). It was a turning point in the development of the Ballets Russes. Nijinsky, the star dancer of the company, and the darling of the company's business manager Diaghilev, devised for his debut a new dancing technique, derived from the paintings on Greek vases and Egyptian friezes. As on the vases the dancers' trunk was turned towards the audience and heads and limbs were in profile. Because of the use of parallel leg positions and a twisted torso, the effect was almost two-dimensional. Audiences found it rather strange, but were particularly upset by the fact that at the conclusion of the ballet Nijinsky played with a veil as if he were masturbating with it. In 1919 Nijinsky's career came to an end when he was diagnosed as schizophrenic. His wife, a Hungarian countess, took him to various psychiatric clinics in Europe, in the hope of finding a doctor who could cure her husband – but to no avail.

True connoisseurs of art, finally, will be bound to come up with the name of the American performance artist Vito Acconci (1940–). In the late 1960s he began using performances, film and video as tools for self-analysis and interpersonal relations. In the mid-1970s Acconci converted exhibition spaces into public meeting places with audio and video installations. A central part of the performances was generally a direct confrontation with the viewer, usually in a very intrusive way. In *Seedbed* (1972) Acconci lay under a floor in a New York gallery. He masturbated for eight hours a day for a total of three weeks, while he spoke his fantasies about the visitors as they walked across the floor: 'you're pushing your cunt down my mouth' and 'you're ramming your cock into my ass'. Pretty daring stuff, certainly, though he did keep hidden . . .

11

In Conclusion

To ask questions about masturbation is at the same time to answer them. Down the centuries a chain of imposed norms, control and intervention, both appropriate and inappropriate, has been imposed. In that context it might have been better to opt for discretion. I could, to quote the philosopher Foucault, have relinquished the 'determined will to know'. However, in retrospect I do not regret my decision to go into the phenomenon more deeply. But as to abolishing the taboo? I soon abandoned that idea.

What does the result of my in-depth study amount to? Well, the long story begins essentially at the beginning of the seventeenth century with a London quack, a surgeon, who practised totally without opposition and whose sole aim with his terrifying tales of masturbation was financial gain. Subsequently it was the universally respected physician Tissot who took up the baton and developed scientific theories, which were then more or less uncritically accepted. Philosophers like Rousseau, Kant and other luminaries of the Enlightenment assisted him in this. 'A sensible person should keep control of his or her body,' was one of the mottos of the Enlightenment. In this scheme of things masturbation was inappropriate and was banned. The Christian Church played a relatively passive role in all this. Things continued in this way up to the end of the nineteenth century: children particularly undoubtedly suffered greatly both physically and mentally from the absurd assumptions of doctors and pedagogues.

Great scholars like Havelock Ellis and Freud finally questioned Tissot's legacy. By the beginning of the twentieth century the majority of doctors had fortunately become convinced that masturbation was basically a harmless pursuit. Apart from that they had been given much more important matters to deal with: the development of anaesthetics, for example, made extensive surgical treatment possible, something that was very necessary in Western Europe, especially after the First World War.

A new Tissot will probably never arise. Or will he? It is true that in the twenty-first century masturbation has climbed to new heights. The internet, which acts as a kind of modern confessional, has opened the way to a virtually anonymous but unlimited platform for triggering impulses and exchanging fantasies among virtual communities of masturbators, as far as we know most of them male.

Obsessive internet reports, rich in detail, today act as a verbal safety valve for the repression of all kinds of sexual feelings. Doctors and confessors have long since been left far behind! Petty and precise sexual teachings have long since ceased to be relevant to much of society. In contrast to the current assumption of the anti-porn movements that 'pornography is the theory and rape is the practice', one is bound to conclude that the activity most encouraged and triggered by pornography is masturbation.

Morality

On the internet one can see all kinds of things – amateur teenagers, live reality, lesbian, gay, mature, extreme, as one umbrella site promises. At the computer screen only one thing usually happens. 'Remember to keep your keyboard clean, they're a bitch to sanitize' reads a tip on one site. 'Masturbation is healthy' is the new motto. According to some people you can even bring world peace closer by doing it. 'War can wait, masturbate' is one of the slogans on www. masturbateforpeace.com. And you can even lose weight . . .

A survey conducted by the American news site MSNBC shows that a third of internet users regularly visit sex sites. Twenty per cent of that number spend over eleven hours a week on it. In 1 per cent of cases there is a serious psychological abnormality. Another large-scale survey revealed that in a single month the five most popular sex sites in the US attracted almost 10 million visitors. The number of internet users in the month when the survey was conducted was 57 million. That means that almost 17 per cent of all users visited one of the five sex sites, quite apart from the hundreds of thousands of other porn pages.

Despite the growth in the number of sex sites, profits are not rising exponentially, because more and more free sites are constantly appearing. At first 1 in 100 visitors spent money, but that figure has fallen to 1 in 400. Some porn companies, by the way, are very smart at winning customers. They lure unsuspecting internet users step by step to their porn sites. That happens to 40 per cent of internet users at some time or other. There have even been a number of legal actions against porn entrepreneurs who gave their sites the names of popular children's series, with a minor change in spelling, like teltubbies.com.

It emerges that men look at completely different things from women. Men look mainly at porn, while women look for new facts to improve their sex lives or breathe new life into it. According to MSNBC men spend on average more time on 'erotic' use of the internet than women: women spend slightly under two hours, men slightly over three hours a week.

In this book many paeans of praise have been sung to masturbation, but the fact is that as a result of the huge quantity of porn available via the internet there are masturbation addicts. Marriages break up because men creep out of bed at night, penis in hand, and sit in front of the computer. In addiction treatment, therapeutic programmes are devised. Another potential risk of the *pornofication* of our society is that young people will again become frightened. They see attractive people doing very exciting things and realize that they are generally uglier and will never have such superb sex. Porn removes sex from the realm of human relationships and locates it purely in the genitalia and in mechanical movements – potentially damaging, in particular for young people.

British philosopher Roger Scruton, author of the book *Beauty*, uses Plato to analyse such contemporary issues as what he calls sex with the Self. In his view a narcissistic, introverted form of sex arises in modern man, who has failed socially. In an interview with a weekly newspaper in July 2009 he said:

> In sexual desire there is always an element of intentionality that is not satisfied by the sexual act. It goes further, towards a longing to be united with the Other. Anyone who cuts the cord, damages himself and the other. Masturbation is a form of cutting the cord, as is compulsive viewing of pornography. Everyone can see that that is morally damaging: not only the narcissistic aspect, but also the shutting off of yourself; it destroys the possibility of having sex with another person.

The large-scale opinion polls quoted in this book regarding people's sex lives confirm that virtually 100 per cent of men and over 80 per cent of women admit to occasionally masturbating. By way of comparison, in the 1940s and 1950s those figures were 90 and 60 per cent respectively. The changed figures are partly the result of pornofication. The main aid to masturbation is the computer, the device that has encouraged masturbation in recent decades.

According to American media philosopher Greg Tuck (quoted in Attwood 2009) both men and women are being reduced to their bodies by pornography and hence being prompted to engage in direct sexual gratification of their needs. Combined with the ancient taboo on masturbation, that might explain why among young men having a large number of sexual contacts is regarded as 'macho', while admitting that you jerk off is 'not done'. If young men want sex, that is seen in our society as natural instead of an autonomous decision. 'Boys will be boys', it is often said – not least by young women. They, however, are regarded as autonomous individuals, since it is up to them to indicate whether or not they want sex. So the double morality in relation to women is a logical consequence: if a woman does not set boundaries to the urges the man displays – and hence fails to act as an autonomous individual – she is immediately condemned. No blame attaches to the man: he is determined 'externally' by his passions, and 'can't help it'.

Secondary schoolteachers would therefore be wise, in their attempt to make young people more resistant to pornography, not to focus first and foremost in their lessons on the objectification of girls into sex objects, as is the case in pornography, but to concentrate mainly on the way in which young men are reduced by porn image culture to their sexual urges. The bringing of masturbation out into the open as a subject of discussion could make a positive contribution: it would enable young people to see masturbation as a normal part of a rich sex life instead of an activity that only distracts from sexual intercourse. Or, in other words, it could encourage young men not to make the gratification of their needs the sole responsibility of women or define their 'masculinity' solely in terms of how many sex partners they have had.

Taboo

In order to become adults we have to acquire a large spectrum of skills. For example we have to learn how to behave sexually, alone and/or with one or more partners. Some people go on to draw the conclusion that masturbation, because it has to be learnt, should also be taught as a skill. But that does not follow at all. We learn many skills that we need to master better – or sometimes only – if we do it in our own way and in our own time, at the moment that suits us. Masturbation is such a skill par excellence: graphic instruction is not necessary. While 'learning on the job' a simple booklet may serve a turn, but it is not indispensable.

Of all sexual actions, masturbation remains the most difficult one to discuss openly. When it is good it is a strictly personal experience, which many people have learned quite wrongly is dirty, sinful, shameful or even unhealthy. It is, however, the most common human sexual expression and is perfectly normal. Why do we do it? Is it because sex with our partner does not satisfy us? Because there is no partner? Because men watch porn and can't contain themselves? Because women read exciting, erotic books? Is it a universal physical need? In my view none of those questions are very relevant. Masturbation is not at any rate a hobby of profligate, hedonistic individualists. 'The cranking up of the machine is a thing in itself, without a moral component or a double bottom. Nothing to worry your head about', as one novelist put it. Masturbation is relaxing for both men and women and acts as an excellent soporific, without side effects. Apart from that, it is free. But most people don't feeling like giving personal details. Replying to my not exactly innocent question about how often she masturbated, a very proper Calvinist acquaintance of mine said that she refused to answer, 'in the same way that she wouldn't give me her pin code'. There's no arguing with that!

Evolutionary biologists see masturbation as an important aid in what is called the 'sperm competition'. Sperm cells that have been stored for too long start to show abnormalities, for example abnormal heads, or no heads at all. For that reason a regular turnover – of between three and five days, it is estimated – is important in the context of reproduction. If that, for whatever reason, is not possible through sexual intercourse, masturbation offers a way out. However, daily masturbation is not sensible, because in that case the number of sperm cells per millilitre falls too sharply.

It will never be possible to prove it scientifically, but masturbation may also be a contraceptive device, a safety valve preventing all kinds of sex crime. One only understands that fully when one knows the kinds of fantasy that accompany many people's masturbation. This fact has scarcely penetrated our society.

After studying the subject of masturbation intensively, I remain in certain respects dissatisfied. Why is the phenomenon still stigmatized in certain circles? Why is masturbation still associated with feelings of guilt, loneliness and shame, even among medical students? There is a very long history behind this. Again and again masturbation was put in the dock, not only by doctors and representatives of religions, but especially by Enlightenment philosophers. Turning masturbation into a problem is the downside of the period in which the modern world has its roots: parallel with the rise of reason and science and the awakening of the autonomous individual, masturbation was characterized as a dangerous, sinful, selfish act. During the entire previous period – in antiquity, the Judaic and Christian world – it was too minor an issue to worry about. It was considered a humdrum, rather obscure activity, which carried no severe moral charge. Long ago that was undoubtedly connected with the suppression of female sexuality, but that time has long since passed.

Whereas writers and poets usually offer consolation when it comes to the 'condition humaine', our laborious toiling beneath the sun and our fretful existence, the vast majority have nothing to say about masturbation. Most just waffle, groan and fret.

Isn't it wonderful that visual artists offer not only consolation but also beauty! In the course of history they have painted marvellous works, especially of masturbating women. I kept a tally for my completely arbitrarily chosen paintings: both female and male subjects used the left hand as often as the right. But that is a minor detail.

Are there other possible steps that can be taken to prevent people agonizing about masturbation? Yes, simple sex education from parents, whether or not with the support of a booklet or a good internet site, a few lessons at secondary school, and perhaps it would make good sense also in the education of social workers, nurses, doctors and psychologists to have a few lectures on evolutionary biology, since it is clear from that science that masturbation is not only a pleasurable but also a very meaningful activity.

Perhaps masturbation in a sociological sense is comparable with the ambivalent stigmatization of the single individual as opposed to the individual in a permanent relationship. The former is not only pathetic because he or she lacks love and care, but is also selfish. The same thing may apply to the adult masturbator: they are alone, pathetic *and* selfish. That applies of course to both men and women.

I fear that for many people it will be a long time before they achieve non-compulsive, fantasy-filled masturbation. The same applies to adequate sex education for our children. It will definitely never reach the point where masturbation lessons take their place alongside swimming and traffic-awareness lessons. That can only happen when we have left behind the eternal glorification of sex issuing in sexual intercourse behind us. That attempt is no doubt doomed to failure. The reality is that the number of singles is rising. Masturbation has a deeply murky past, but solitary sex has a 'golden future' ahead of it.

Bibliographical Sources

Aaron, Jean-Paul and Roger Kempf, *Le Pénis et la démoralisation de l'Occident* (Paris, 1978)

Adler, Otto, *Die Mangelhafte Geschlechtsempfindung des Weibes* (Berlin, 1904)

Altmann, A., *Lexikon Kulturgeschichte, Literatur und Kunst, Sexualwissenschaft: herausgegeben vom Institut für Sexualforschung in Wien* (Hamburg, 1961)

Andahazi, Federico, *The Anatomist* (New York, 1998)

Anon., *Seksuele taboes in Nederland. De resultaten van een grootschalig onderzoek naar seksuele taboes in Nederland* (Amsterdam, 2003)

Attwood, Feona, *Mainstreaming Sex: the Sexualisation of Western Culture* (London, 2009)

Baker, Robert R. and Mark A. Bellis, *Human Sperm Competition* (London, 1995)

Bataille, Georges, *Story of the Eye* (London, 1979)

Battaglia, Cesare, Rossella Elena Nappi, Fulvia Mancini, Arianna Cianciosi, Nicola Persico, Paolo Busacchi, 'Ultrasonographic and Doppler Findings of Subclinical Clitoral Microtraumatisms in Mountain Bikers and Horseback Riders', *Journal of Sexual Medicine*, VI (2009), pp. 464–8

Bauer, L., 'Infibulation as a Remedy for Epilepsy and Seminal Losses', *St. Louis Clinical Record*, VI (1879), pp. 163–5

Bennet, Paula and Vernon A. Rosario, *Solitary Pleasures: The Historical, Literary and Artistic Discourses of Autoeroticism* (New York, 1995)

Bockting, W. O. and E. Coleman, *Masturbation as a Means of Achieving Sexual Health* (New York, 2002)

Bonnetain, Paul, *Charlot s'amuse* (Geneva, 1883)

Braun, Gustav, *Compendium der Frauenkrankheiten* (Vienna, 1863)

Brody, Stuart, 'Slimness is Associated with Greater Intercourse and Lesser Masturbation Frequency', *Journal of Sex and Marital Therapy*, XXX (2004), pp. 251–61

—, 'Blood Pressure Reactivity to Stress Is Better for People Who Recently Had Penile-vaginal Intercourse than for People Who Had Other or No Sexual

Activity', *Biological Psychology*, LXXI (2006), pp. 214–22

—, 'Intercourse Orgasm Consistency, Concordances of Women's Genital And Subjective Arousal, and Erotic Stimulus Presentation Sequence', *Journal of Sex and Marital Therapy*, XXXIII (2007), pp. 31–9

Brody, Stuart and Rui Miguel Costa, 'Vaginal Orgasm Is Associated with Less Use of Immature Psychological Defence Mechanisms', *Journal of Sexual Medicine*, VI (2009), pp. 464–8

Brody, Stuart and Tilman H. Krüger, 'The Post-orgasmic Prolactin Increase Following Intercourse Is Greater than Following Masturbation and Suggests Greater Satiety', *Biological Psychology*, LXXI (2006), pp. 312–15

Castelot, André, *Marie Antoinette* (Paris, 1962)

Céline, Louis-Ferdinand, *Journey to the End of the Night*, (trans. Ralph Manheim (London, 1991)

Chang, Jolan, *The Tao of Love and Sex* (London, 1991)

Columbus, Renaldus, *De Re Anatomica* (Venice, 1559)

Delfos, Martine, *Zin in jezelf: Seksuele voorlichting over masturbatie* (Bussum, 1999)

Dixson, Alan F., *Primate Sexuality: Comparative Studies of the Prosiminians, Monkeys, Apes, and Human Beings* (Oxford, 1998)

Dodson, Betty, *Sex for One: The Joy of Selfloving* (New York, 1996)

Drenth, Jelto, *The Origin of the World* (London, 2004)

—, www.melsvandriel.com

Ellis, Havelock, *Studies in the Psychology of Sex* (New York, 1936)

Emin, Tracey, *A Thousand Drawings* (London, 2009)

Ensler, Eve, *The Vagina Monologues* (London, 2001)

Euridice, *F/32* (Boulder, CO, Normal, IL, and Brooklyn, NY, 1990)

Faust, B.C., *Verhandeling weegens een noodzakelyke verbeetering der kleeding. Met eene voorrede van J.H.J. Campe. Uit het Hoogduitsch vertaald, en met aanmerkingen vermeerderd, door W. G. Beneevens en BRIEF en AANMERKINGEN van H. A. Bake, M. D. over dit Werkje, waarin de beoordeling van hetzelfde* (Amsterdam, 1792)

Fliedl, Gottfried, *Gustav Klimt, 1862–1918. The World in Female Form* (Cologne, 2006)

Ford, Clellan S. and Frank A. Beach, *Patterns of Sexual Behaviour* (London, 1952)

Freud, Sigmund, *Drei Abhandlungen zur Sexualtheorie*, 6th edn (Vienna, 1926)

Fuchs, Eduard, *Geschichte der Erotischen Kunst* (Berlin, 1908)

Goethe, Johann Wolfgang von, *Dichtung und Wahrheit* (Leipzig, 1928)

—, *Erotic Poems*, trans. D. Luke (Oxford, 1997)

Gorky, Maxim, *Bystander (The Life of Klim Samgin)* vol. I, trans. Bernard Guilbert Guerney (London, 1930)

Graber, B. and G. Kline-Graber, 'Female Orgasm: Role of the Pubococygeus.' *Journal of Clinical Psychiatry*, XXX (1979), pp. 34–9

Halpert, E., 'On a Particular Form of Masturbation in Women: Masturbation with Water', *Journal of the American Psychoanalytic Association*, XXI (1973), p. 526

Hammond, William A., *Sexual Impotence in the Male and Female* (New York, 1974)

Hansen, J. K. and T. Balslev, 'Hand Activities in Infantile Masturbation: A Video Analysis of 13 Cases', *European Pediatric Neurology* (13 Nov. 2008)

Häring, Bernhard, *Das Gesetz Christi* (Freiburg, 1967)

Herbenick, Debra, Michael Reece, Stephanie Sanders, Brian Dodge, Annahita Ghassemi, J. Dennis Fortenberry, 'Prevalence and Characteristics of Vibrator Use by Women in the United States: Results from a Nationally Representative Study', *Journal of Sexual Medicine*, VI (2009), pp. 1857–66

Hite, Shere, *The Hite Report on Male Sexuality* (New York, 1981)

Houellebecq, Michel, *Atomised*, trans. Frank Wynne (London, 2001)

Imami, R. H. and M. Kemal, 'Vacuum Cleaner Use in Autoerotic Death', *American Journal of Forensic Medicine and Pathology*, IX (1988), pp. 246–8

Jacobi, A., 'On masturbation and hysteria in young children', *American Journal of Obstetrics and Diseases of Women and Children*, VIII (1876), pp. 595–606

Jacoby, S., 'Sex in America', *AARP: The Magazine*, CXIV (July–August 2005) pp. 57–62

Joyce, James, *Ulysses* (London, 1960)

Judson, Olivia, *Dr Tatiana's Sex Advice to all Creation: The Definitive Guide to the Evolutionary Biology of Sex* (London, 2003)

Kant, Immanuel, *Traité de pédagogie* (Paris, 1886)

Keesey, Douglas and Paul Duncan, *Erotic Cinema* (Cologne, 2005)

Kellogg, J. H., *Plain Facts for Old and Young* (Burlington, VT, 1888)

Kinsey, Alfred C., W. B. Pomeroy and C. E. Martin, *Sexual Behaviour in the Male* (Philadelphia, PA, 1947)

Kitzinger, Sheila, *Women's Experience of Sex* (Harmondsworth, 1985)

Koornstra, Jan J. and Rinse Weersema, 'Management of Rectal Foreign Bodies: Description of a New Technique and Clinical Practice Guidelines', *World Journal of Gastroenterology*, XIV (2008), pp. 4403–6

Krenkel, Werner A., 'Masturbation in der Antike', *Wissenschaftliche Zeitschrift der Wilhelm-Pieck Universität Rostock*, XXIX (1979), pp. 159–72

Larivaille, Paul, *La vie quotidienne en Italie au temps de Machiavel* (Paris, 1979)

Laqueur, Thomas W., *Making Sex: Body and Gender from the Greeks to Freud* (Ambridge, PA, 1990)

—, *Solitary Sex: A Cultural History of Masturbation* (New York, 2003)

Legman, G., *Rationale of the Dirty Joke: An Analysis of Sexual Humor* (New York, 1968)

—, *The New Limerick: 2750 Examples American and British* (London, 1978)

Leitzman, M. F., A. Platz, M. J. Stampfer, W. C. Willett and E. Giovannucci,

'Ejaculation frequency and subsequent risk of prostate cancer', *Journal of the American Medical Association*, CCXCI (2004), pp. 1578–86

Licht, Hans, *Das Liebesleben der Griechen* (Dresden and Zurich, 1926)

Maines, Rachel, *The Technology of Orgasm* (Baltimore, MD, 1999)

Marten, John, *Onania, or the Heinous Sin of Self-Pollution and All its Frightful Consequences* (London, 1712)

Marton, R. B., *Erotika Biblion* (London, 1605)

Masters, William H. and Virginia E. Johnson, *Human Sexual Response* (New York, 1966)

—, *Human Sexual Inadequacy* (New York, 1970)

McCourt, Frank, *Angela's Ashes* (London, 1997)

Mead, Ralph and Christian Snyder, *The Sole Sex Joke Book* (Mobile, AL, 1999)

Meizner, Israel, 'Sonographic Observation of in utero Fetal "Masturbation" ', *Journal of Ultrasound in Medicine*, VI (1987), III, p. 111.

Miersch, Michael, *Das bizarre Sexualleben der Tiere* (Munich, 2002)

Moravia, Alberto, *The Two of Us*, trans. Angus Davidson (London, 1974)

Morvincit, A., *Schadelijke of onschadelijk? Nieuwe inzichten over een oud erotisch vraagstuk* (Leiden, 1925)

Mountjoy, P. T., 'Some Early Attempts to Modify Penile Erection in Horse and Human: An Historical Analysis', *Psychological Record*, XXIV (1974), pp. 291–308

Muthesius, Angelika, Burkhard Riemschneider and Gilles Néret, *Twentieth-Century Erotic Art* (Cologne, 1998)

Onfray, Michel, *Antimanuel de philosophie: leçons socratiques ert alternatives* (Paris, 2001)

Paton, W. R., trans. and ed., *The Greek Anthology* (London, 1916), vol. I

Peleg, R. and A. Peleg, 'Sexual Intercourse as a Potential Treatment for Intractable Hiccups', *Canadian Family Physician*, XLVI (2000), pp. 1631–2

Pouillet, Theodore, 'L'Onanisme chez la Femme' (Paris, 1880)

Ranke-Heinemann, Uta, *Eunuchs for the Kingdom of Heaven: Women, Sexuality and the Catholic Church*, trans. P. Heinegg (New York, 1991)

Roach, Mary, *Bonk* (New York, 2008)

Robertson, A., 'Notes of a visit to American lunatic asylums', *Journal of Mental Science*, XV (1969), pp. 49–89

Roche, Charlotte, *Wetlands* (London, 2009)

Rousseau, Jean-Jacques, *Confessions*, trans. Angela Scholar (Oxford, 2000)

—, *The Social Contract*, trans. G.D.H. Cole (1913), available at www.constitution.org/jjr/socon/htm, accessed September 2011

Schoondermark, Jr, J., *Het auto en mutueel onaneeren van mannen en jongens en vrouwen en meisjes, zijne gevolgen, en zijne behandeling. En opstel voor 'rijp en groen'* (Amsterdam, 1902)

Scruton, Roger, *Beauty* (Oxford, 2009)

—, *Sexual Desire: A Philosophical Investigation* (London, 2006)

Shokeir, A. A. and M. I. Hussein, 'Sexual Life in Pharaonic Egypt: Towards a Urological View', *International Journal of Impotence Research*, XVI (2004), pp. 385–6

Sullivan, J. P. and A. J. Boyle, eds, *Martial in English* (Harmondsworth, 1996)

Swift, Rachel, *Woman's Pleasure, or How to Have an Orgasm as Often as You Want* (London, 1993)

Szasz, Thomas, *Sex by Prescription. The Startling Truth about Today's Sex Therapy* (Syracuse, NY, 1990)

Tissot, Samuel A., *Traité de l'Onanisme: Dissertation sur les maladies produites par la masturbation* (Lausanne, 1760)

Toole, John Kennedy, *A Confederacy of Dunces* (Harmondsworth, 1981)

Twain, Mark, *Some Remarks on the Science of Onanism*, in Mark Twain, *The Mammoth God, an Address to the Stomach Club* (Waukesha, WI, 1976)

Valente, G., L. Krikhaar and R. Haenen, *Sextoys* (Amersfoort, 2003)

Waxman, Jamye, *Getting Off: A Woman's Guide to Masturbation* (Berkeley, CA, 2007)

Weatherhead, Leslie, *The Mastery of Sex through Philosophy and Religion* (London, 1933)

Weldon, Fay, *Leader of the Band* (London, 1988)

Yellowlees, D., 'Masturbation', *Journal of Mental Science*, XXII (1876), pp. 336–7

—, 'Masturbation', in *Dictionary of Psychological Medicine*, ed. D. H. Tuke (London, 1892)

Zaviačič, Milan, *The Human Female Prostate* (Bratislava, 1999)

Photo Acknowledgements

The author and the publishers wish to express their thanks to the below sources of illustrative material and/or permission to reproduce it:

Albertina, Vienna: p. 224; © The Trustees of the British Museum: p. 147; © DACS 2012: p. 225 top; © Salvador Dalí Fundació Gala-Salvador Dalí, DACS, 2012: p. 226; Collection Mels van Driel, Eelde: p. 222; © Tracey Emin. All rights reserved, DACS 2012: p. 229; © Eric Fischl: p. 227; Gemäldegalerie, Dresden: p. 211; Kunsthistorisches Museum, Vienna: p. 219; By permission of Jordan McKenzie: p. 231; National Museum, Athens: p. 210: Private Collection, Vienna: p. 301; Rijksmuseum, Amsterdam: p. 216; © Christian Schad Stiftung Aschaffenburg / VG Bild-Kunst, Bonn and DACS, London 2012: p. 225 bottom; The State Hermitage Museum, St Petersburg: p. 215; Collection Robert Walker: p. 220; Windsor Castle, Royal Library, copyright Her Majesty Queen Elizabeth II: p. 38.

Index